'This book laid bare my paltry u[...]ing[...]of the p[...]; mercy. Natalie writes with the raw honesty and authenticity of an individual who has been both the recipient of and a participant in God's mercy, and has been radically transformed in the process. This book will inspire and challenge you to rediscover that mercy is at the heart of our spiritual formation.'
Olivia Amartey, Executive Director, Elim

'An incredible read! Nat has thrown a javelin right into the heart of one of the main tenets of people of the Way: mercy. Without it, we miss out on the dignity and freedom it is bestowed for.

Jesus + mercy = God's "A game" for humanity, so we reflect his fullest nature and character. Mercy is an adventure – not for the faint-hearted, but for the brave!'
Tarn Bright, CEO, Home for Good

'*'Tis Mercy All* is a beautifully written book packed with honesty, encouragement and conviction. It stirs the heart and mind to not only understand and receive the wonder of God's mercy towards us, but also the call as receivers to share this mercy with others. This book is already having an impact on my life, and I look forward to reading it again.'
Lou Fellingham, worship leader

'Natalie's previous book gave a frank assessment of the UK Church that had me nodding and clapping in agreement. *'Tis Mercy All* gives me the opportunity to look inwardly in a way that is at times uncomfortable, but is a necessary assessment of self as we seek to know and be more like our Lord Christ Jesus.'
Tola-Doll Fisher, author and editor of Premier's *Woman Alive* magazine

'Reading this beautiful book will mean you encounter wave after wave of the mercy of God for yourself. Such is the revelation of what

God has done for us in Christ, and how kindly he has treated us, that you can't help but be swept up in wanting to show that same mercy to others.'
Abi Flavell, Catalyst Network of Churches

'In this timely and honest book, laced with biblical insights, Natalie takes a deep dive into God's mercy, giving us a prophetic challenge that is coupled with practical tools to think and act mercifully. A brilliant and accessible book that helped me glimpse God's mercy afresh.'
Andy Frost, Director, Share Jesus, and Joint CEO, Gather Movement

'*Tis Mercy All* is a prophetic cry for the Church to grasp the transformative beauty and power of mercy. Natalie masterfully builds, thread by thread, a rich tapestry of what mercy is, why we should rejoice in it, and how we must spread it around. A timely and compelling book for the simple but often-disregarded truth that mercy changes everything.'
Jo Frost, co-author of *Being Human*, Director of Communications and Engagement, Evangelical Alliance

'With biblical truth, lived experience and practical wisdom, Natalie Williams calls the Church, and indeed all people, back to a fuller definition of biblical mercy and loving-kindness. This book shows the heart of God towards his creation, and especially humanity. The mandate to all is clear: we should go and do likewise.'
Pastor Tope Koleoso, Jubilee Church London

'Imagine the Bible's message as a beautiful piece of music conveying God's saving love to humanity. If justice is the "bass-line", then surely mercy is the soaring melody. The mercy of Jesus is breathtaking: able to reach deep into our broken world and damaged souls, and to offer the redemption we could never achieve for ourselves.

'But aren't justice and mercy in tension with each other? How can they be part of the same tune? Showing how justice and mercy can be harmonised and enhance each other is the great strength of Natalie Williams's latest book, *'Tis Mercy All*. As she argues, we should be angry about the terrible injustices that scar our world and work against them with all our might.

'But our indignation must never eclipse the immense, overwhelming mercy of God. We must continually remember that we all sin and fall short, we are all complicit and need mercy. In a world eager to 'cancel' those who transgress, Christians should never lose the humility that comes from wisdom.

'Natalie's theology has been hammered out on the coalface of addressing poverty in her local community. This is the kind of theology we need: integrated, practical and lived. Read this book, dig deep into the mercy of God, and be inspired to live it out!'
Jon Kuhrt, CEO, Hope into Action

'In a world where anger and demands for justice often drown out calls for compassion, Natalie's book delivers a vital message of biblical, loving mercy. Through her skilful weaving together of Scripture and lived experience, Natalie challenges and uplifts, reminding us of the transformative power of mercy.

'I was personally impacted by the book's relevance to the issues we face in our daily work at London City Mission. I highly recommend it to all who long to see the world impacted for Christ. This is a much-needed book from an important voice for our times.'
Graham Miller, Chief Executive, London City Mission

'Natalie is a woman who models mercy. In this personal, hard-hitting, yet very accessible book, she challenges believers to live in a gospel-centred, countercultural way by extending God's mercy to our broken world. It is biblical, practical and brutally honest.'
Guy Miller, Commission Apostolic Trust

'Natalie's deep insights into the Scriptures will stir you afresh to serve others in the name of the God who is rich in mercy. They will also sustain your spirit to keep on serving in the face of every difficulty you encounter along the way. Essential reading for anybody who wants to partner with God in serving others.'
Phil Moore, author of the *Straight to the Heart* series of Bible commentaries and of *The Forgotten Manifesto of Jesus*

'Throughout reading this book, I found myself with a long list of "buts": "but not this person", "but not this unconditionally", "but…". As Natalie unpeeled the layers of God's mercy, my "buts" began to have to be put away. I realised how selectively I apply God's mercy – to myself and to others – and how much more I want the mercy I offer to look like God's.

'This book made mercy three-dimensional and stretched my thinking in each of those dimensions! Prepare for it to be one of those books you will need to come back to again and again, as we let the truth of God's mercy change, challenge and inspire us.'
Kat Osborn, CEO, Safe Families

'I'm a huge fan of Natalie's heart, voice and work, but even so I found myself frequently astonished at the depths and riches of this wonderful book. It represents a three-strand cord of biblical exposition, Holy Spirit revelation and lived experience that will stir your heart, shape your life and move your hands and feet towards God and the people he loves. As you read about the extravagance of God's mercy, and as Natalie guides you through the most difficult questions, may you be astounded again at the incomparable love of Jesus and the riches of grace that are ours, and ours to share.'
Akhtar Shah, The Foundry and Kingdom Embassy

'*Tis Mercy All* is one of the most provocative books I've read in a long time. Nat takes us on her personal journey of discovering God's mercy – which is both brutally honest and disarmingly inspirational. As the beauty of God's heart of mercy unfolds before us, we find ourselves propelled into acting mercifully towards others.

'This book will not only expand your understanding of God's mercy, it will change your life!'
Jeremy Simpkins, ChristCentral Churches

'Natalie Williams presents a gloriously rich view of God's mercy. Gleaned from the full canon of Scripture, the depth, breadth and wonder of mercy is on display. This is an incredibly generous work, laced with humility and honest self-reflection. As ever, Natalie grounds her teaching in relevant application that exhorts readers to offer their lives mercifully to the outcast and the overlooked, the cancelled and the condemned. This is a great read!'
Sam Ward, UK CEO, The Message Trust

'This is a bright, vivid presentation of one of Scripture's most wonderful themes: the mercy of God towards us, and its implications for the mercy we show to each other. *'Tis Mercy All* is challenging, yet encouraging; moving, yet refreshing; theologically rich, yet practically accessible.'
Andrew Wilson, Teaching Pastor, King's Church London

'No one can read this book and doubt that Natalie Williams is utterly sold out for Jesus. In a world in which differing opinions and careless mistakes get us cancelled, Natalie has other ideas. With heart-wrenching examples of grace so momentous it could only be powered by God, Natalie walks us through our need to show mercy, and also to receive it. She doesn't pretend it's easy. This isn't a 'wear your best smile on a Sunday' faith; this is a gritty, determined faith that says, "I'll never be strong enough to do this without you, Jesus." This is a book we all need, and thankfully now we've got it.'
Lauren Windle, author of *Notes on Love* and *Notes on Feminism*

Natalie Williams (@natwillnatter) grew up in a working-class family in Hastings, one of the most deprived towns in England. She worked as a journalist and has co-authored three books about how Christians in the UK can respond to poverty: *The Myth of the Undeserving Poor* (2014); *A Church for the Poor* (2017); *A Call to Act* (2020); and a book about class issues in the Church, *Invisible Divides* (2022). Natalie is Chief Executive of the charity Jubilee+, which equips churches to change the lives of those in poverty in their communities (@jubileeplus).

'TIS MERCY ALL

The power of mercy in a polarised world

Natalie Williams

First published in Great Britain in 2024

SPCK
SPCK Group
Studio 101
The Record Hall
16–16A Baldwin's Gardens
London EC1N 7RJ
www.spckpublishing.co.uk

British Library Cataloguing-in-Publication Data
A catalogue record for this book is available from the British Library

ISBN 978–0–281–08918–5
eBook ISBN 978–0–281–08919–2
Audio ISBN 978–0–281–08920–8

1 3 5 7 9 10 8 6 4 2

Typeset by Fakenham Prepress Solutions
First printed in Great Britain by Clays Ltd

eBook by Fakenham Prepress Solutions

Produced on paper from sustainable sources

'Tis mercy all! Let earth adore,
Let angel minds inquire no more...
...'Tis mercy all, immense and free;
For, O my God, it found out me.
Charles Wesley[1]

We know that the true story of our life, when known, will prove to be,
as the hymn says, 'mercy from first to last' – and we are content.
J. I. Packer[2]

Jesus,
Lord of my life and love of my life,
your mercy towards me is magnificent.
This book is for you.
I have sought to find words of delight
to proclaim your excellencies.
My deepest desire is that it would bring great joy to your heart,
just as your immense mercy has brought such joy to mine.
Thank you for letting me write it.

Contents

Contents

Acknowledgements

I imagined I would write this book in my old age, when I had learned everything there is to know about the mercy of God. But I got here early, through a strange trial that plunged me deep into my Father's mercies in a vibrant, tender and powerful way. The message of God's mercy started to feel like there was 'in my heart... a burning fire shut up in my bones' (Jeremiah 20:9) that I could not hold in.

My friends Jeremy Simpkins and Ginny Burgin were the first to tell me to get on with it. Then, after a brief conversation at a conference, Terry Virgo told me he had been unable to stop thinking about my mercy book that morning, and he thought I should write it without delay. So I did – with gratitude to the three who gently pushed me into it much sooner than I had planned.

Readers of early drafts – Nigel Ring, Richard Wilson, Martin Charlesworth, Michelle Earwaker and Carlo Galluzzo – gave me really valuable feedback and spurred me on. Special thanks are due to Phil Moore, who was incredibly generous with his time, and brought insight and clarity to me as we pored over the draft together. Phil, thank you – the book is far better for your input; you helped me to make it the book I wanted it to be.

I am grateful to Elizabeth Neep at SPCK, who believed in this from the start, and to my editor, Joy Tibbs, for catching the heart of this book and sharpening my writing so I could communicate it more effectively. Thanks also to Paul and Charlotte Braithwaite for allowing me to tell part of your story.

Lots of lovely people have committed to pray for me: Pete and Sue Lyndon, Mike Gale, and my WhatsApp prayer warriors. Thank you for faithfully holding me, and this book, up to God.

Acknowledgements

I am also blessed to work with exceptional people at Jubilee+. The core team, directors and staff make it a joy to lead. Thanks also to friends of J+ who came to our Prayer and Prophecy Day and prayed with energy for this project. Special thanks to my brilliant PA, Ailsa Magee. Without your incredible skill at shuffling commitments in my diary, this book would not have been finished. Thank you for bringing order to my chaos.

God has given me way more than my fair share of wonderful friends. My cup overflows! It is one of his greatest mercies to me. I can't mention all who are dear to me, but I do want to thank those who have been very much on 'the mercy book' journey with me.

Sunday nights joking about my future Winnebago, watching hit-and-miss TV series, and eating Paul's 'cooking' may not be good for my body, but they are a joy to my soul. Paul and Chloe Mann, Brian Marriott and Jo Gobbett, thanks for all the fun.

Andrew Bunt, it's an honour to sit beside you on God's mercy seat!

Hannah Beaney, I am grateful for your steadiness and humour over many years of friendship. How about you read this one?

Anna Heasman, thanks for the Ashburnham walks and letting me muscle in on your family holidays!

Mark Evetts, thank you for always pointing me to the Wonderful Counsellor.

Michelle 'Meesh' Earwaker, no one makes me laugh as much as you do. Thanks for all the road trips, and for always cheering me on.

Joanna Mutu, thank you for always asking after my heart. It adores Jesus more because of you.

Liz Pursglove, your faithful friendship tethered me to the mercies of God when I felt adrift. Thank you for walking beside me in the valley and constantly reminding me to fix my gaze on Jesus.

Richard and Anna Wilson, thank you for helping me to eat well, think biblically and work out what it means to love mercy.

Mum, you are resilient, steadfast and funny. Thank you for all you have taught me about grit and tenacity. Jesus really loves you.

Introduction

My friend Jo was killed by a lorry driver while she was cycling to work. She was thirty-four.

The driver was reversing his 14-tonne lorry – a cement mixer – around a corner when he hit her. He was arrested for causing death by careless driving. His vehicle had three mirrors on the left side, so there was no blind spot. He had no excuse. He had simply, and tragically, failed to pay proper attention. He did not see Jo on her bike, despite other drivers sounding their horns and pedestrians trying to alert him.

After pleading guilty, the driver was warned by the judge that he faced a custodial sentence – he was likely to go to prison. But between the verdict and the sentencing, Jo's parents, Paul and Charlotte, wrote to the judge, asking him to show mercy.

Because of this, the judge didn't send the driver to jail. He relented, saying, 'They do not seek retribution and have recognised how this has affected you.'

Isn't that incredible? If Jo were my daughter, I'm pretty sure I would not have been thinking about how the driver was affected. I would have been more concerned with how *I* was affected!

The driver could have been given the maximum sentence of five years in prison. However, my friend's parents extended mercy to the man who had caused their daughter's death. As a result, he was given a suspended sentence and community work, and was banned from driving for three years. There were consequences for his actions – in losing his driving licence he lost his livelihood of forty-three years – but he was shown mercy.[1]

National and local media covered the outcome of the court case. One newspaper headline read: 'Death driver shown mercy.'

1

It made national news because mercy of this magnitude is rare in society today. In fact, mercy of any magnitude is scarce. We live in an increasingly polarised world, where even hearing the word 'mercy' is uncommon. So when we hear about it, it is powerful, it is challenging, and sometimes it is even offensive. We want justice, not mercy, and we struggle to see how both can exist in the same space.

This is true even in the Church, where we should be intimately acquainted with both the mercy of God and his call on us to be mercy-bringers to those around us. I often have the privilege of speaking to congregations on this subject. Whenever I include the story of Paul and Charlotte's mercy towards the lorry driver, people respond with astonished gasps. We are amazed. We haven't heard many mercy stories like this, much less seen mercy demonstrated in our day-to-day lives.

But even radical, undeserved, costly mercy like this should not be so rare among us as followers of Jesus, who have received mercy through Christ's death on the cross. It should be a defining characteristic of who we are. It should set us apart from the society around us and cause people to look on in wonder. It should be one of the primary ways people see Jesus through us.

In my early years as a Christian, I often heard mercy described as being spared a deserved punishment (as in the case of the driver who caused Jo's death). Mercy definitely is that, but I believe it is bigger and broader and deeper and richer. There are three Hebrew words in the Old Testament that can be rendered as 'mercy': *rakham*, *khannun* and *khesed* – and most English versions of the Bible translate all three as 'mercy' in some verses.[2] In the Greek New Testament, the word 'mercy' is always derived from a single word, *eleos*, but each of the Hebrew words can be accurately translated as 'mercy', depending on the context.[3]

These various words show us that biblical mercy is about much more than escaping punishment. It overlaps with grace, steadfast love and compassion, with unfathomable kindness and abundant generosity. This is what we see throughout Scripture: evil tyrant kings are shown the kind of mercy that withholds the wrath they deserve (Manasseh in 2 Chronicles 33), and a young virgin girl is shown the kind of mercy that bestows upon her the incredible gift of bearing, raising, mothering and loving the Son of God (Mary in Luke 1:26–55).

A better definition of mercy goes beyond sparing someone the judgement they deserve. It conveys something far more active, far more abundant. Biblical mercy is loving-kindness in action towards someone who does not deserve it. It is active compassion towards those who have no right to demand it, no credible claim to it, and no reason to expect it.

Though the driver did not ask Jo's parents to forgive him, they approached him after the court hearing to assure him of their forgiveness. Extending mercy did not take away their pain, but they were able to offer it in such a profound and moving way because they had already received it themselves. Because they knew the merciful God revealed in the Bible, they were able to do as Jesus instructed: 'Be merciful, just as your Father is merciful' (Luke 6:36, NIV).

And we can too. The world around us needs us to do so.

Anti-mercy

Most of us will never have to apply it at such a profound level as Paul and Charlotte, but there are areas where we all struggle to live up to this incredible call to be merciful, just as God is merciful. I know I do. It's hard. When I pay attention to the attitudes and reactions in my heart, I find I am prone to being judgemental, not merciful. If your church ran a course on how to be more judgemental, I would not need to attend. It comes quite naturally to me!

Mercy, however, needs work. It needs cultivating. I have to push and be pushed to lean towards it. Left to my own devices, I default to judgement. But that's not my job. Judgement is reserved for God. Jesus told his disciples not to judge. Instead, we are to be merciful. This is a wonderful invitation from Jesus to be like our Father – to carry the family resemblance and impact the world around us with a mercy that is unfathomable to most.

But to be honest with you, I do not always like mercy. Don't get me wrong – if you come to my church and say, 'Hands up who likes mercy', I'm going to raise my hand. I like it when it is shown to *me*. But when I clock some of the attitudes that come out of my mouth and reactions that flash up in my heart, I realise I am not so keen on mercy when it is shown to those who, in my opinion, do not deserve it.

Because the thing is, mercy is not fair, and I like things to be fair. Mercy absolves people of the punishment they deserve (or we believe they deserve). Mercy gives people things they haven't earned. Mercy doesn't treat people based on what they have done or failed to do. I'm delighted when it's applied to me, but not so happy when it's applied to those who jumped ahead in life because they were born into the right family; those who cheated their way to the top and cannot be toppled; those who hurt me and didn't seem to care; those who looked out for themselves to the detriment of others. I could go on.

Getting what you deserve – that makes sense to me.

Earning what you have – that makes sense to me.

But mercy is not a meritocracy.

Most of us like to believe that any achievement in our lives is down to us – that we had some part to play in our success – and that any failing is due to circumstances beyond our control. How easily we flip this when it comes to other people. We find ourselves believing that those who are less successful didn't try hard enough. If all it takes to succeed is hard work and applying oneself, they must be architects of their own failure.

But the mercy of God is a great leveller. When we grasp it, we see that none of us deserves the things that matter: love, forgiveness, kindness... even life itself.

The world around us is sorely and sadly lacking in mercy. We see it in cancel culture, where no apology or atonement is sufficient to deal with our present or past sins. We see it in virtue signalling, where we race to let everyone know we are on the 'right' side, denouncing those who deserve vitriol from those of us who are enlightened. We see it in our politics, where nuance and cross-party collaboration have been largely cast aside, and those who disagree with us become our arch-enemies, in whom there is no good.

No wonder King David said he would rather fall into the hands of God than people, 'for his mercy is very great' (1 Chronicles 21:13; 2 Samuel 24:14). Conversely, Romans 1:21–31 concludes its long list of the behaviours that characterise the unrighteous with 'they have... no mercy' (NIV).

And that's what we see on display in the world around us: 'no mercy'.

It is not that our culture simply lacks mercy.

It's that it is *anti-mercy*.

Our fallen humanity pits mercy against justice and concludes that mercy minimises the harm done to us and requires us to deny or even hide wickedness. We define other people by their sins, assuming evil intent on their part, while defining ourselves by the sins committed against us, defending our own mistakes by claiming that our motives were good. Our culture tells us that apologies and attempts to atone for wrongdoings cannot be trusted. We are told that our treatment of others should be based on whether they deserve it, how they treat us, and if they are grateful enough. Social media reminds us not to cross an ocean for someone who would not cross a puddle for us. Self-care is the highest priority. Charity begins at home. Look out for number one.

Even to Christian ears, this may sound reasonable.

But it is not the Jesus way.

Followers of Christ are called to live lives of radical, countercultural, sacrificial mercy, shaped not by the world around us or the person in front of us, but by who God is and how he acts towards us.

We are called by Jesus himself to be merciful like our Father.

We are to be characterised by a mercy that reflects the heart of God – a mercy the world cannot offer.

The gulf between God's mercy and ours is enormous. In many respects that is inevitable – he is God and we are not – but when it comes to being merciful, too often I look more like the world around me than the One who sent his Son to save me.

Before we figure out how to become more like our Father, we need to dwell deeply on his mercy towards us. It is only when we start to grasp that *'tis mercy all*, from first to last in how God treats us, that we can hope to emulate him – or we even want to.

So before we get into what it means to live a life of mercy, we'll use Part 1 to take a deep dive into God's mercy towards us, reflecting on it from multiple angles. If you start to wonder why I'm devoting so many words to this, it's because we are so slow to really get it. We fall quickly into imagining God is angry towards, displeased with, disappointed in or exasperated by us. We have taught ourselves to hear him sighing over us rather than singing over us. We need to marinate in his mercy until it reaches the deepest recesses of our hearts and minds.

In Part 2 we will start to explore *why* we struggle to comprehend the richness of God's mercy. We are so conditioned by the way the world is, and by the way we are, that even when we begin to see how merciful God is, we're slow to accept it. If mercy is not visible in the culture around us, and barely evident in our own hearts, can God *really* be that wonderfully kind, forgiving, relenting, restoring, patient, steadfast and compassionate? If we have never seen anything like it, perhaps it's too good to be true. We tend to slip into seeing God as we are – making him in our image, rather than seeing him as he really is. Or we struggle to get our heads around the fact that some of his other attributes, such as holiness, justice and anger, do not negate his mercy but reveal it to be all the more astounding.

It is only once we have been wowed by the mercy of God that we can be wooed into a life of mercy. This starts with our attitudes, then our actions catch up. We need to start thinking like God, but thinking mercifully requires us to acknowledge and dismantle the ways in which our thoughts are not like his. So in Part 3 we will unpick some of our unmerciful thinking. It won't be comfortable, but if we are willing to be honest and repent of where our thinking is far from God's, it will be transformative. We will begin to see ourselves and others the way Jesus sees people, and this will take us on the exciting adventure of becoming more merciful.

In Part 4 we will turn our attention to what it looks like to act mercifully. Once we have started to understand how wonderfully merciful the Father is in all his dealings with us (yes, *all* of them!) and have begun to align our thoughts with his, we will be changed. We will cultivate not just hearts and minds that are merciful, but also hands, feet, homes and even bank balances.

When it comes to the God of the Bible, it really *'tis mercy all*, from first to last. When we realise that, we will be radically transformed into followers of Jesus who become mercy-bringers to a world that so desperately needs to know mercy.

Part 1
'A GOD MERCIFUL'

I started going to church because I liked a boy. I wasn't thinking about becoming a Christian. I wasn't interested in Jesus, the Bible or anything to do with God. I wasn't seeking anything spiritual at all. I was fourteen and I had a crush on a boy, and that was it. But from my first Sunday at church, I was intrigued. Nothing about the service was what I expected it to be. I thought church was for elderly people. I was a teenager when I first went along, and the biggest surprise was that there were lots of people my age there.

I embarked on my journey into faith without really knowing what was happening. To be honest, it felt as if it happened *to me*, rather than being due to any intentionality on my part. In the six months between first visiting the church and eventually praying a prayer to accept Jesus as my Lord and Saviour, I struggled to figure out what God was like so that I could decide if I actually wanted to believe in, let alone follow, him.

Initially, I was wrestling with a god I didn't even believe in. I had a very clear idea about what this imaginary god was like: he was uncaring, harsh and mean. I didn't like him, and I was adamant that I didn't want anything to do with him.

A few months later, having become a church-attending atheist wondering about faith, I stood in the middle of the vast local crematorium. As I stared at the little plaque marking my brother's very short life and premature death, I asked, and argued with, God about what he is like. What sort of god lets babies die for no reason? And more than that, what sort of god lets a baby die knowing the deep and devastating ripple effect it will have on his family for decades to come?

Just as it is for many people, my path to becoming a Christian was fraught with intense questions about suffering, unfairness and death. And the truth is, I didn't become a Christian because my questions were answered, or even because I'd made peace with them, but simply because I had started to believe – despite my best resistance – that God was actually real, and I couldn't see a way back once I knew that.

Before I started following Jesus, I wrestled with God over his nature, his character. And thirty years later, that has continued to be the biggest struggle of my Christian life: believing that God is not mean, but merciful. He really is good. He is kind, compassionate and tender-hearted. He loves me, wants the very best for me, and works all things for my good. It is true – incredibly, wonderfully, magnificently true – but believing it doesn't always come easily.

The glory of God

I wonder if it was the same for Moses. In Exodus 33:18 (NIV) we read that Moses said to God: 'Now show me your glory.' It recently dawned on me what an especially odd request this was when one of my church pastors pointed out that, at the time of asking, Moses had already seen God speak to him from a burning bush, send ten plagues on Egypt, part the Red Sea, rain down bread from heaven, provide water from a rock, and plenty more besides. Hadn't Moses repeatedly seen God's glory?

It seems unnecessary, almost irreverent, for Moses to request this after everything he had seen God do. It sounds a little demanding, even brazen. Perhaps he expected God to show his glory by flinging some new stars into the night sky and revealing himself to be the mighty, all-powerful Creator of the universe. Or maybe Moses thought God would create a new animal or plant right in front of him, demonstrating that he is the One who makes all things. Or perhaps he expected God to roar like thunder and lightning, splitting and shaking the ground on which he stood.

God could have done any of these things to show Moses his glory. He had already caused the sea to partition into walls so Moses and the Israelites could walk through on dry ground. He could have responded by picking up a mountain and setting it down in a different location.

But instead of moving a mountain, God Almighty, 'the Father of glory' (Ephesians 1:17), invited Moses to come up a mountain and meet with him. And up there on Mount Sinai, God revealed his glory: '[I am] a God merciful and gracious, slow to anger, and abounding in steadfast love and faithfulness' (Exodus 34:6).

'A God merciful...'

Pause for a moment and contemplate how extraordinary that is. God's glory can be seen in his power, his wisdom, his holiness. It is displayed through all his attributes – it's evident in all his ways and all his works. But here, when Moses got as close to God as anyone could before Jesus came, we see that God's primary way of identifying and describing himself is as 'a God merciful'.

God could have dazzled Moses with a display of his might and power. Instead, his magnificence is in his mercy.

Moses had encountered the voice of God, the presence of God and the power of God. Yet here, in this precious, personal moment on the mountain, we find that God's glory is not primarily found in his *greatness*, but in his *goodness*.

God is not mean. He is merciful. It is who he is. And it is still how he reveals his glory today, to us.

1

Rich in mercy

I once hurt a dear friend deeply by saying something offensive about her parents. I hadn't meant it the way it came out. I was clumsy with my words, and my friend was rightly angry with me. But as we tried to talk it through, I could see that no matter how much I apologised, she wasn't going to be able to let it go – not that evening, at least. And as it turned out, not for a long while. She did eventually forgive me, but it took months to persuade her that I was genuinely sorry.

It often feels as though this is how it is with God. We sin, either by doing something we shouldn't or not doing something we should, and then we feel like we need to work our way back into God's favour. We expect a probation period before we can be fully restored, like an ice hockey player relegated to the 'sin bin' for a suitable time out. We know God is forgiving, we know he is merciful, but we feel like we've got to earn it – at least a little bit. That's the way of the world. An apology is not enough. We have to mean it. More than that, we have to *prove* we mean it.

But that's not how it is with God.

The Bible says that God is 'rich in mercy' (Ephesians 2:4).

Rich. Not stingy, not lacking, not tight-fisted.

His mercy isn't meagre or sparse. It is abundant, and he loves to pour it out.

But rich mercy is so foreign to us that we struggle to get our heads around it. When I do something wrong, I slide straight into thinking that I need to nag and cajole God into showing me mercy. I think I need to twist his arm, forgetting he is more loving than I dare to hope.

Think back to the day you first encountered God. You came to him through his mercy. You didn't have anything to offer him, other than your sin. Whatever path you took in coming to know Christ as your Lord and Saviour, the place we all first meet him is at the cross. Jesus died for us when we did not deserve it and could not earn it. We were not simply uninterested; we were enemies of God (Romans 5:10). We were deserving of wrath (Ephesians 2:3). Yet while we were still sinners, Jesus died in our place (Romans 5:8).

I find it much easier to believe in the mercy I first encountered at the cross than in the ongoing mercy of God when I mess up. But the truth is, God was merciful the day he saved me, he has been merciful every day since, and he'll be merciful every day ahead. He is not hard-hearted, even when I am.

He is rich in mercy.

Recalling Jesus' words

I think the apostle Peter demonstrated a clear grasp of this after denying Jesus. In the final chapter of John's Gospel, we read that Peter decided to go fishing and some of the other disciples went with him. While they were out on the boat, they saw Jesus standing on the shore. John 21:7 tells us: 'When Simon Peter heard that it was the Lord, he… threw himself into the sea.' Peter wanted to get to Jesus as quickly as possible. The funny thing is, the boat was only 100 yards out… but Peter couldn't wait!

Think about it for a moment. Peter had denied knowing Jesus. He had failed the Lord he loved. When Jesus told him this would happen, Peter protested. He said that even if all the other disciples fell away, he would be the one still standing. He assured Jesus that he wouldn't deny him, even if it cost him his life (Mark 14:27–31).

Have you ever gone over and over a conversation in your head? I often do that. I like words. Words of affirmation are my love language, so I memorise kind and encouraging words. But I also replay hurtful words. I can recall painful conversations long after they happened and – to my detriment, and often the pain of the other person – bring up specific words by way of accusation: 'But you said…' Words really matter to me.

I wonder what it was like for Peter in those days between denying Jesus and having breakfast with him on the beach. I wonder which conversations he replayed over and over in his head. Remember, Peter would have heard Jesus say: 'Whoever denies me before men, I also will deny him before my Father who is in heaven' (Matthew 10:33). No wonder Peter broke down and wept bitterly once he had denied knowing Jesus three times (Matthew 26:75).

But Peter had heard other words he could call to mind: 'As the Father has loved me, so have I loved you' (John 15:9). Peter had heard Jesus speak powerful words of love and forgiveness, and he had seen Jesus in action. He knew that Jesus had compassion on the crowds and showed mercy towards sinners. Jesus had told Peter personally: 'I have prayed for you that your faith may not fail. And when you have turned again, strengthen your brothers' (Luke 22:31–32).

Peter knew that Jesus loved him.

I wonder if Peter threw himself off the boat to get to Jesus because he knew that Jesus, being fully God, the perfect representation of his Father, was rich in mercy. Because he had seen enough to know Jesus' heart.

Have we?

The lack of mercy in the world around us can so easily seep into our thinking, causing us to question whether God could really be so quick to forgive. Could he truly be that kind, that patient, that tender-hearted towards us?

As Sam Storms writes in his book *A Dozen Things God Did with Your Sin*: 'We are all capable at times of showing mercy to those in need. But our mercy is all too often measured and calculated. God is "rich" in mercy! His mercy is abundant and overflowing and never comes piecemeal.'[1]

Throughout the Bible, God is lavish with his mercy. He isn't stingy with it. He doesn't ration it, doling out a little here and there, only when we've grovelled enough or tried to make it up to him.

'Nowhere else in the Bible is God described as rich in anything,' writes Dane Ortlund. 'The only thing he is called *rich* in is: mercy.'[2]

The God who revealed himself to Moses as 'a God merciful' is not reluctant to show mercy to us.

He is rich in mercy.

2

Unrestrained mercy

On the rare occasions when there are glimmers of mercy in the world around us, it is unshakably conditional: *If you do something wrong, we will only consider showing you mercy if you are sorry. Not just that, but you need to prove you are sorry. Also, you need to not make the same mistakes again.*

The world's propensity for forgiveness is limited, to say the least. Just hop on to social media on any given day to see the wolves circling the latest public figure who has said or done something they shouldn't have. It happens in the Church, too. When a high-profile American pastor confessed to sending 'inappropriate' Instagram messages to a woman in his church, and said he would take a leave of absence, many Christians took to X (formerly Twitter) to denounce him. The tone, in general, was that 'there's no smoke without fire' and 'more scandal must be about to break'.

Of course, both may well be true. But the point is that the immediate reaction, even among many Christians, was to assume the worst. The pastor did something wrong, by his own admission, and so, on social media at least, we pour out judgement and withhold mercy, just like the world around us.

Maybe this pastor doesn't deserve mercy, you might argue.

I agree completely.

But neither do you. Neither do I.

Our desire for repentance is godly. Our desire for justice is godly. These are right responses to wrong things. They are part of how we reflect the image of God, who is perfect and pure and cannot tolerate evil.

But followers of Jesus are also called to 'love mercy' and 'be merciful' (Micah 6:8; Luke 6:36, NIV).

So how does that work? How do we hold these things in tension?

The truth is, we usually don't. We tend to lurch in one direction, because simultaneously acting justly and loving mercy is complicated and sometimes paradoxical. It feels too difficult. We withhold mercy, keeping it pent up behind a dam, imagining that unrestrained mercy will sweep away justice like a flood. We believe that to show mercy would be to minimise the harm done to us, so we demand justice and despise mercy.[1]

When I read the story of the prodigal son in Luke's Gospel, I am well aware that I wouldn't welcome the son back the way the father does. I want mercy to be withheld. Not forever, necessarily, but definitely for a while. I want the son to have a period of penance – a long one! – during which he can reflect on the damage he has caused, and sit for a time with the consequences of his actions. But the father in the parable doesn't even wait to hear what the son has to say. He rushes to his wayward son, throws his arms around him and kisses him. He doesn't know if the son is even remotely sorry!

Neither do we. All we know is that he reached a place of desperation, knowing he would starve if he didn't do something. We have no idea if he expressed true repentance *before* his father welcomed him home. All we know for certain is that he came up with some words that he thought might be persuasive enough for his dad to let him return as a servant. His motivation, as far as we can tell from the text, was food. Of course, it's possible that the prodigal son was genuinely repentant, but there's no hard evidence of that. I'd apologise for anything if I was hungry enough!

When I do something wrong and it causes a minor or major catastrophe in my life, I often find it hard to know if I am really sorry, or just sorry because of the consequences. Maybe no one except God, who knows our hearts, could truly know whether the prodigal was repentant or just desperate for food. Whatever his motives, the prodigal receives instant and unwavering mercy from the father figure in the story. The father doesn't withhold mercy. He actually *runs* to show his son mercy.

How far this is from my usual perception of God when I've sinned! But the father in the parable represents God. Jesus is telling us a story about his Father, *our* Father.

Just as he is *rich* in mercy, God is *unrestrained* in mercy.

Even when we mess up time and time again, God does not withhold his mercy from us.

We see this throughout the Bible, but I love the particular expression of it in Psalm 40:11–12, where David is honest about his sin, writing: 'For evils have encompassed me beyond number; my iniquities have overtaken me, and I cannot see; they are more than the hairs of my head; my heart fails me.'

Have you ever felt like that? In my thirty years as a Christian, I have had a few occasions when I've become so painfully aware of my sinfulness that I feel swamped by it, soaked in it, overwhelmed by it. At those times, which are mercifully few and far between, I feel like I'm drowning in my sin and cannot see beyond it.

Yet before David openly proclaims the awful extent of his sin, he also proclaims: 'As for you, O LORD, you will not restrain your mercy from me; your steadfast love and your faithfulness will ever preserve me!'

When we feel overwhelmed by our sinfulness, we need to lift our eyes away from ourselves.

I should know better by now.

Yes.

I've fallen in the same area a dozen times before.

Yes.

A hundred times.

Yes.

My sins feel vast as the ocean.

Yes.

Recognising and acknowledging our sinfulness is good. But if we focus our attention there, we end up in the quicksand of condemnation. If we linger, we sink.

If God's mercy towards me is based on my sins, or lack of them, I'm in serious trouble. So are you.

If his mercy is subject to how well I am performing as a Christian, there is no hope for me.

The Bible is very clear that God's mercy is dependent on *him*, not you or me. In fact, in Galatians 3, the apostle Paul says I am 'foolish' and 'cursed' when I start to believe that my 'works' can earn God's grace. Even my repentance is granted to me as a gift from God – initiated by him, not me (Acts 11:18; 2 Timothy 2:25).

God is merciful because it is who he is. He doesn't just *show* mercy; he *is* mercy.

And his mercy doesn't wax and wane according to our behaviour. It is fixed.

There is no such thing as mercy that is deserved. Merited mercy is an oxymoron. If I had a right to it, or any claim on it at all, it would not be mercy.

It is as simple and hard to fathom as this: no matter what we have done or failed to do, God promises not to withhold mercy from us when we cry out to him.

3

Relentless mercy

All sorts of things can bring a smile to my face. Some may be expected, such as a beautiful sunset. Others bring me what some might say is an odd amount of joy, such as a properly used semicolon and hard-to-track-down cinnamon Turkish Delight.

Do you ever wonder what makes God happy?

Jesus is so often depicted in art and on screen as looking very serious and sombre. He is portrayed as a 'man of sorrows' (Isaiah 53:3), which he was, but nowhere near as much airtime is given to the fact that he was also 'anointed... with the oil of joy' (Hebrews 1:9, NASB).

Jesus was acquainted with grief, but he wasn't miserable. God is not unhappy.

But what makes him happy? What brings him joy?

One answer can be found in the words of the prophet Micah, who writes: 'Who is a God like you, who pardons sin and forgives the transgression of the remnant of his inheritance? You do not stay angry for ever but delight to show mercy' (Micah 7:18, NIV).

God *delights* in showing mercy.

Pause for a second to deeply inhale this beautiful truth.

God *delights* in showing mercy.

He wants to be merciful to us. It brings him joy!

I find it relatively easy to believe that God was delighted to show me mercy when I first came to him. But I find it much harder to believe that he finds joy in showing me mercy today. He saved me many years ago, yet some days I think and act as if I'm still a baby Christian, and that feels like failure. For one thing, I still break the Ten Commandments. Even though I've walked with Jesus for three decades, I don't seem to be able to keep any of them permanently, at least not in the light of how Jesus talks about them as matters of the heart during his Sermon on the Mount (Matthew 5:21–28).

I know that I am no longer a slave to sin, and that I am clothed in the righteousness of Christ. I am being sanctified: my desire for Jesus is growing while my desire for sin is shrinking. But I still sin all the time, especially when it comes to heart attitudes. Little sins. Big sins. One-off sins. Habitual sins. Obvious sins. Secret sins. Wilful sins and those committed in ignorance. Even when I'm doing pretty well at resisting temptation, I can end up sinning by feeling proud and self-righteous about it!

The more mature I become in my faith, the more I can relate to David, who revealed in his psalms that he was increasingly and painfully aware of his sin (for example in Psalm 51:3–4).

As we grow in appreciation for God's holiness, we become more and more aware of how wayward we are. This awareness of sin is good – *if* it leads us to a deeper revelation of God's mercy. That's what it is designed to do. It is only when we recognise our dire predicament that we can stand in awe of the relentless mercy of God towards us. To deny our sinfulness is to be like the Pharisees. But we must not swing to the other extreme either. We need a healthy awareness of our sin – knowing that we have been washed clean by the blood of Jesus and are now saints who sometimes sin, but are not enslaved by it; yet also growing in our awareness of the depths of our sin and how desperately we need the mercy of God.

God *delights* in showing mercy.

Astonishingly, he so enjoys showing us mercy that he does it every day: 'The steadfast love of the LORD never ceases; his mercies never come to an end; they are new every morning; great is your faithfulness' (Lamentations 3:22–23).

They are new every morning.

Every single day, he has new mercies for us.

'He has no off days and no half-hearted days,' writes David

Gibson. 'No days where instead of pursuit he dawdles in his goodness or forgets to follow in his mercy.'[1]

Aren't you grateful? I know I am.

Nevertheless, God...

This book would be a lot longer if I listed all my sins in it, and would probably run to volumes if my friends and family added to the list. We have an example of this in Psalm 106, where verse after verse recounts the sins of God's people. They carried out wickedness, failed to consider or remember God's works, rebelled, forgot, did not wait, put God to the test, were jealous, worshipped idols, despised the promise of God, had no faith, complained, disobeyed, yoked themselves to false gods, provoked God to anger, and even sacrificed their children. But keep reading and get this: *nevertheless* he delivered them many times, heard their cries, remembered his covenant, relented and kept his steadfast love and mercy towards them. As Ortlund says in response to this psalm: '[God] enjoys washing sinners in a flood of love and mercy. This is who he is.'[2]

We are slow to understand that God's mercy is relentless. But he has given us plenty of examples of it in the Bible. If what we read in Psalm 106 is not enough, we can turn to Nehemiah 9 to find another long list of the waywardness of God's people, who were in the habit of turning back to him only when they suffered distress because of their sins. Yet every instance of their iniquity is met with the beautiful refrain that God, in his 'great mercies', was faithful to them (Nehemiah 9:19–31).

When I see the ocean of my sin, the only thing that stands between that sight and crushing condemnation is the overflowing, abundant mercy of God.

My sin is no match for his mercy.

My sin is no match for his mercy!

It's marvellous. This is why the gospel is 'good news'!

But we can so easily miss it.

The Bible calls the devil our accuser (Revelation 12:10), because he accuses us day and night, pointing out our sins and failings to God. His accusations may well be accurate – most likely, they are – but it doesn't matter because God sees all our transgressions. He knows the depravity of our hearts, our selfishness, our pride and our self-absorption. Yet *he delights in showing mercy*!

He so delights in doing it that he went to excruciatingly painful lengths so we could be redeemed, cleansed and forgiven. In 2 Samuel 14:14 it says that God 'devises means so that the banished one will not remain an outcast'. I love that. God *devises* ways to save us. It makes me think of him planning and plotting the various ways in which he will come to your rescue and mine.

The Father wants us. He devises ways to mercifully make us his own. He devised *the* way to deal with our sin justly and mercifully so we could belong to him, purchased by the blood of Jesus, adopted into his family.

The Father sent his Son as a ransom for me. He silences the accuser and trades my filthy rags for spotless robes of righteousness (Zechariah 3:1–5; Revelation 19:7–8).

So, though I still sin, there is fresh mercy for me every day.

In the context of writing about weakness, sin and temptation, the author of the letter to the Hebrews affirms: 'Let us then with confidence draw near to the throne of grace, that we may receive mercy and find grace to help in time of need' (Hebrews 4:16).

Followers of Jesus are assured that we will find mercy when we need it. It's guaranteed. It seems too good to be true, yet it is. From God's rich supply, which he delights in dispensing to us every single day, we find ourselves overwhelmed by wave upon wave of his relentless mercy.

Every drop of sin has been covered by the blood of Jesus. Not one speck or dot remains. The vast chasm that sat, gaping wide, between God and us has been filled to overflowing with the beautiful, relentless, delightful mercy of God.

Because Jesus died in our place, the only chasm that remains is the one between us and our sin:

So great is His mercy toward those who fear Him;
As far as the east is from the west,
So far has He removed our transgressions from us.
(Psalm 103:10–12, NKJV)

No wonder the author of Lamentations writes: 'But this I call to mind, and therefore I have hope' (Lamentations 3:21).

On the rare occasions when the world around us does offer mercy, it is finite. We are fortunate if we get three strikes before we're out. But God's mercy is limitless. The Bible repeatedly tells us that God's mercy is unending. Just spend some time in Psalm 136 in the New King James Version, and you will be immersed in the truth that 'His mercy endures forever'.[3]

For followers of Jesus, trying to out-sin God's mercy is like King Canute trying to hold back the tide.[4] God's mercy woos and pursues us. It comes to find us and bring us back when we go astray like stupid sheep. When David writes in Psalm 23:6 that 'surely goodness and mercy shall follow' him all the days of his life, the word 'follow' is a weak rendering of the Hebrew. David Gibson explains: 'Goodness and mercy pursue David; they do not merely follow him. The word is so intensive, it is often used in combat scenes, where people are "pursued" to death... [David] knows that the "mercy" hot on his heels is the covenant mercy of God... his loving-kindness, his loyal, committed, faithful love.'[5]

Unlike the world's mercy, which is hard-fought, hard-won and only given if we can make a case that we deserve it, God's mercy sees us as we really are, and relentlessly envelops us anyway.

We may not see it, and we may even try to run away from it. Even so, the mercy of God towards us never runs out.

Amazingly, it even runs after us.

4

Jesus, the merciful One

There is no greater demonstration of God's mercy than the cross of Jesus Christ. If the continuous refrain through the pages of Scripture is *'tis mercy all* from first to last, the wooden cross on which Jesus died is the crescendo.

The cross reveals powerfully, unequivocally, that God will go to extraordinary measures to show us mercy. But it also reveals just as profoundly that our sin is no joke.

If a deep dive into his mercy leads us to be glib about sin – to think we can do whatever we want and it doesn't matter because God will show us mercy anyway – then we have totally and utterly missed it, and we would be wise to question whether we really know Jesus.

My experience is the complete opposite: the more I contemplate how merciful God has been to me, the more I want to live a life that brings glory and honour to his name. We need not fear that dwelling on the riches of his mercy will make us complacent, flippant or prone to stumbling into sin without concern. No! The more we see his mercy, the more we see our sin in all its ugliness. And the more we see our sin, the more we wonder at his marvellous mercy towards us.

Mercy doesn't give us licence to sin. It is 'in view of God's mercy' that we offer ourselves fully to God 'as a living sacrifice, holy and pleasing' to him (Romans 12:1, NIV). God's kindness doesn't lead us to sin; it leads us to repentance (Romans 2:4). Revelation of his mercy isn't a gateway to wickedness; it is the door through which we receive healing for our waywardness (Hosea 14:3–4a, NKJV).

Mercy changes us

Nowhere is this more clearly demonstrated than in the life of Jesus. Those who encountered his mercy were radically transformed. As Jesus welcomed, forgave and embraced those who recognised their sin and their need of a saviour, the trajectory of their lives was changed.

Take the woman who entered the home of Simon the Pharisee with her alabaster flask of ointment and anointed Jesus. We are told she was 'a woman of the city, who was a sinner', and Simon judged Jesus for not knowing 'what sort of woman this is who is touching him' (Luke 7:37, 39). Of course, Jesus absolutely knew all about the woman – he did not deny that she had sinned, nor did he give any excuses or mitigating circumstances for her sin. In fact, he acknowledged that her sins 'are many' (Luke 7:47). But in his mercy, he did not define her as 'a woman of the city' or a sinner. Instead, Jesus sees her as forgiven, generous and loving (Luke 7:44–50). Centuries on, she is still remembered. She has become known to generations of believers not as an infamous sinner, but as a beautiful worshipper.

One of the clearest ways we see the mercy of Jesus at work is through the company he kept. He spent time with people no one else wanted to hang out with – in fact, the very people others avoided. Our culture is one in which we keep our distance from certain people. We see it when politicians, celebrities, sports stars or even church leaders fall into disrepute. When the misdeeds of the famous are exposed, people associated with them often run for the hills. In the age of social media, this usually involves public denouncement and distancing.

Wonderfully, powerfully, beautifully, this is not the way of Jesus. With radically countercultural mercy, he does the exact opposite: he walks towards, draws near to and befriends those from whom others run. As Dane Ortlund writes: 'Time and again it is the morally disgusting, the socially reviled, the inexcusable and undeserving, who do not simply receive Christ's mercy but *to whom Christ most naturally gravitates.*'[1]

Jesus touches the unclean, eats with the unsavoury and walks into the no-go areas. He lets his own reputation be tarnished by the reputations of those around him, even to the point of being called 'a glutton and a drunkard, a friend of tax collectors and sinners!' (Matthew 11:19).

I love this about Jesus. I love the fact that he hangs out with sinners and outcasts, because that's how I see myself. When I read the Gospels, I usually cast myself in the role of the disciples or those who came to Jesus knowing their need of him.

But Jesus also ate with Pharisees, praised the faith of a Roman centurion, and invited himself to dinner with the chief tax collector, Zacchaeus, who had become wealthy by exploiting and defrauding his fellow Jews. Just as it would have been scandalous to the Pharisees for Jesus to enter the home of tax collectors and sinners, so it would have been scandalous to his disciples for Jesus to show mercy to those (Jewish or otherwise) who were oppressing the Jews.

I definitely feel more comfortable with the Jesus who sat down to eat with Simon the leper than I do with the Jesus who shared a meal with Simon the Pharisee.[2] And I prefer the idea of Jesus sitting on the pavement sharing a McDonald's with someone who is homeless to the thought of him dining in the home of a wealthy politician who doesn't seem to care about the plight of the poorest. I want Jesus to invest his time, energy and compassion in victims rather than perpetrators.

But in the Gospels we read about Jesus reaching out to both. If the Pharisees and scribes are presented as the 'bad guys' – those who Jesus himself says do not practise what they preach, who 'tie up heavy burdens, hard to bear, and lay them on people's shoulders, but they themselves are not willing to move them with their finger'

(Matthew 23:4) – what are we to make of Jesus eating in the homes of Pharisees, receiving Nicodemus and Joseph of Arimathea, and, after his resurrection, saving Saul of Tarsus?

Or if the 'bad guys' are the tax collectors, those who were taking money from their own people and working for their oppressors, the Romans, what are we to do with the fact that Jesus ate with Zacchaeus and called Matthew to be one of his closest twelve disciples?

Speaking of the Romans, Jesus was even merciful to them. Though the Jews would have expected the Messiah to forcefully liberate them from their oppressors, we see him healing one of their paralysed servants and praising a centurion's faith (Matthew 8:5–13).

Whomever we think of as the 'bad guys' – the oppressing Romans or religious leaders, the unclean lepers and adulterers, the exploitative tax collectors or people like the Samaritans, from the places we despise – we have to face the fact that Jesus was merciful to people from each of these groups. What's more, he did not seem to care about offending anyone by mixing with their enemies.

Not like us

I struggle with this. I run a charity called Jubilee+, which equips churches to change the lives of those trapped in poverty in their communities. I have spent years cultivating a heart for those in poverty that reflects God's heart (I'm still working on it). I have held meetings with politicians who genuinely believe that people who face financial difficulties do so entirely as a result of their own choices. I have spent time with very wealthy people who, by their own admission, do not want to share what they have. And I am in frequent contact with Christians who believe that only *some* followers of Jesus are called to care about poverty, while the rest are called to other things.

If I got to choose whom Jesus shared food with, whom he healed, whom he picked out of a crowd and beckoned over, I would choose people in need and people like me. Because the truth is, like the Pharisees, I have very clear ideas about whom I think it is appropriate for Jesus to talk to, be kind to, and show mercy to.

But Jesus is not like us. While others were terrified of becoming unclean by being in the vicinity of certain people, Jesus had no such fear. Instead of putting up boundaries between himself and 'undesirables', he tore down barriers. Those who had been excluded from the Jewish temple were welcomed by the Son of God (Matthew 21:12–14). One of the hallmarks of his mercy is that it drew people to him who were hated and ostracised by other 'religious' people.

Jesus spent much of his time with those in chronic need. There were no barriers in terms of age, gender or ethnicity. Jews and Gentiles came to him for help. Samaritans – who were hated by Jews – were not excluded by Jesus. Men were not favoured above women. Children were welcomed as equally worthy of his attention as adults. Jesus interacted with those on the margins of society: spurned prostitutes, unclean lepers, shunned beggars, despised tax collectors, oppressive Roman soldiers and reviled ethnic minorities. Those who were rejected, hated and devalued by others not only felt comfortable around Jesus, but actively sought him out.

Jesus lived out the call he issued to his disciples: he was merciful, just as his Father was merciful. He extended his mercy – his Father's mercy – to all of humanity. Not everyone responded with gratitude or faith, but no one was turned away on the grounds of who they were, or what they had done. Jesus wasn't ignorant of their sins and circumstances. He even knew their thoughts.[3]

But, just like his Father, he acted not in response to the behaviour of those around him, but in accordance with his own character. At all times. *'Tis mercy all.* He knew exactly whom he was eating with, touching, healing, forgiving. He chose to be a friend of sinners. It wasn't accidental or incidental, but deliberate and intentional. Just like his Father, Jesus delights in showing mercy to those whom most people would reject and discard.

Jesus' mercy changes us in ways that no amount of condemnation or judgement could. It is not stoning the adulterous woman that will cause her to leave her life of immorality. It is mercy. It isn't calling out Zacchaeus's sins that leads him from greed and exploitation to repayment and generosity. It is mercy. It is not holding Peter at arms' length that will turn him from a fear-filled denier of Jesus into a faith-filled proclaimer of the gospel. It is mercy.

That is why, when the Pharisees criticised Jesus for eating with sinners, he told them: 'Go and learn what this means: "I desire mercy, and not sacrifice"' (Matthew 9:13). He is calling us to a life of radical mercy, and the starting place is recognising that it is his mercy that has wooed and won us, and is now transforming us into his likeness. We can be sure that the mercy of God is doing exactly the same in the people we would not have chosen.

5

Mercy for all?

'God has mercy on whomever he wills' (Romans 9:18), but the Bible gives no examples of people who cried out to God for mercy and were refused it.

What about the Pharisees? Jesus spoke harsh words to them, but mercy is not always gentle. Contrary to the Christmas carol 'Hark! The Herald Angels Sing', mercy is rarely mild. Sometimes it comes like a slap across the face – as David writes in Psalm 141:5 (NASB): 'May the righteous strike me with mercy and discipline me.' When we look at the character of Jesus in the Gospels as a whole, it's entirely reasonable to assume that the harsh things he said to the Pharisees were motivated by mercy.

But we don't have to assume it. We see it in his clandestine night-time conversation with Nicodemus, where Jesus takes the time to explain the ways of the kingdom of God (John 3). We hear it in his lament over Jerusalem, which comes hot on the heels of multiple rebukes towards the Pharisees, where Jesus repeatedly calls them hypocrites. His words are harsh, but his heart is to gather them to himself (Matthew 23:37).

We also see it in Jesus' final earthly words to his disciples, where he reiterates the Great Commission – calling them first to Jerusalem, the holy city of the Jews. If we remain in any doubt that Jesus' heart was for the Pharisees to receive his mercy, his encounter with Saul on the road to Damascus (Acts 9) shows the lengths he will go to in order to draw even hardened Pharisees to himself. Saul, later known as the apostle Paul, describes himself as 'a Pharisee, a son of Pharisees' (Acts 23:6), 'a Hebrew of Hebrews; as to the law, a Pharisee' (Philippians 3:5), and 'extremely zealous... for the traditions of my fathers' (Galatians 1:14).

Jesus dramatically revealed himself to Saul, who was persecuting him by violently ravaging his Church (Acts 7:58 – 8:3; Galatians 1:13), even travelling to other cities to hunt down Christians and do them harm (Acts 9:1–2). What we see on the Damascus Road is Jesus stopping Saul in his tracks – not in wrath, but in mercy.

Moved to mercy

Even some of the most unspeakably evil characters in the Bible received God's mercy. Manasseh is a prime example. He was the son of Hezekiah, who himself had wandered from God and been drawn back by his mercy (Isaiah 38). Manasseh was still a boy when he became king of Judah, but he reigned for a long time – from the age of twelve to sixty-seven. He put up altars to false gods, even in the house of the Lord, and turned to sorcerers, fortune-tellers and mediums, leading the people of Judah and Jerusalem astray. Manasseh 'did much evil in the sight of the LORD', shedding 'very much innocent blood' and even burning his sons to death (2 Kings 21:9, 16; 2 Chronicles 33:6).

In his mercy, God spoke to Manasseh, but Manasseh ignored him. So God let Manasseh be captured and bound by the king of Assyria. We read that 'when he was in distress, [Manasseh] entreated the favour of the LORD his God' (2 Chronicles 33:12). I bet he did! He had heaped up evil deed after evil deed, drawing others into his wicked ways and ignoring God's voice, yet as soon as he was in distress, Manasseh cried out to God.

I don't know about you, but if I were God, I'd have let him languish. If ever there were a time when it would be appropriate to say: 'You've made your bed, now lie in it...', surely this was it! By anyone's reckoning, Manasseh did not deserve mercy. And yet 'God was moved by his entreaty' (2 Chronicles 33:13) and restored him as king in Jerusalem.

God is wondrously merciful in his dealings with us!

The common factor

Jesus emphasised that God deals with us on the basis of *his* character, not *ours*, when he said that our Father in heaven 'is kind to the ungrateful and the evil' (Luke 6:35).

God truly is merciful to *all* who call on him for help. We see this in concentrated form in Psalm 107, where we meet four groups of distressed people who are crying out to the Lord.

First, we have a group of wanderers in a desert wasteland, where they cannot build homes or find food and drink. They are dying. 'Then they cried out to the LORD in their trouble, and he delivered them from their distress' (Psalm 107:6, NIV).

The second group is sitting in complete darkness; prisoners suffering in iron chains and bitter labour. How did they end up here? They were rebellious towards God and despised his plans, and now they have no one to help them. 'Then they cried to the LORD in their trouble, and he saved them from their distress' (Psalm 107:13, NIV).

Next, we encounter some more rebels. These people have become fools, suffering because of their sins. Like the first group, they are dying, but it is clearly their own fault. Nevertheless, like the hungry wanderers: 'Then they cried to the LORD in their trouble, and he saved them from their distress' (Psalm 107:19, NIV).

Finally, we come across some merchants who are caught up in a storm on their ships. The storm becomes so terrifying that they lose courage and are at their wits' end, not knowing what to do. 'Then they cried out to the LORD in their trouble, and he brought them out of their distress' (Psalm 107:28, NIV).

There are modern-day equivalents of all these groups in our communities today. In the UK and many other Western nations, we have seen a huge rise in the number of food banks, some giving out thousands of food parcels a year to those who would otherwise go hungry. Homelessness is all around us – both seen and unseen – with some sleeping on benches and in doorways, while others sofa-surf or languish in unheated accommodation with damp and mould.

Like the second and third groups in Psalm 107, I'm sure we can all think of people who have found themselves in a desperate place owing to the decisions they've made. Perhaps they are in prison because they committed a crime, in debt because they gambled their money away, or have lost everything because of a substance addiction they initially thought of as a fun and controllable hobby.

Similarly, we all know people who are battered by the storms of life, who can't seem to catch a break and are powerless to change their circumstances. Maybe that's the asylum seeker living in the hostel down the road who was so fearful of staying in their homeland that, having lost loved ones and possessions, they risked their life by crossing land and sea to reach what they hoped might become a safe haven. Or it could be someone suffering with mental illness, someone who has been orphaned, or someone caught in a natural disaster. There are many reasons why people find themselves in a desperate place where they genuinely cannot do anything to get their heads above water.

In Psalm 107, we come across the homeless and hungry, the guilty and imprisoned, the foolish and self-damaged, the storm-battered and sinking. Four groups of people; four different situations; four causes of distress.

But only one response from God.

Mercy.

Tim Keller writes: 'Despite their radically different situations, there was one common factor... Everyone who cried to God was heard. Behold how he loves us.'[1]

When we cry out to God, whether owing to circumstances we cannot control or to our own sinful actions, we can count on him to be moved to mercy towards us. Psalm 107 ends with this: 'Let whoever is wise reflect on these things and understand the merciful love of the Lord' (Psalm 107:43, NCB).

If it seems like I'm labouring the point, I am. You might be thinking, *Yes, yes, God's merciful. We get it, Nat.* But the thing is, we really don't. We need to hear it and read it and be reminded of it over and over again, because we forget so quickly, so easily, that God is more wonderfully merciful, kind, tender, gentle, loving and gracious than we can even begin to comprehend. God's mercy is so extraordinary that we have to knead it deep into our hearts and minds so that our default thought patterns can be challenged, displaced and renewed.

We do not need to wonder how God responds to our distress, whatever its cause, because the Bible is clear that he is consistent in his mercy. We are faithless, but he is faithful. His mercies are more certain than the sunrise and more abundant than drops of water in the ocean.

He heals, satisfies the thirsty, breaks chains, delivers from darkness and stills storms. We get to respond to his mercy in the same way the four groups in Psalm 107 did: by giving thanks for his unfailing love and his wonderful deeds towards us; by praising God 'for his miracle mercy to the children he loves' (Psalm 107:8, MSG); and, like the rebellious ones who were shown mercy despite their foolishness, by declaring his merciful works with rejoicing in the way that only those who really grasp the mercy of God truly can.

But followers of Jesus are not just to live in the good of the mercy we have received, but to share it with others. We are called to love mercy and be merciful – to become mercy-bringers to the world around us.

Loving mercy requires us to *think* differently.

Being merciful requires us to *act* differently.

Before we can do either, we need to explore some of the things that can cause us to struggle with, and even object to, God's mercy.

Part 2

OUR STRUGGLE TO 'LOVE MERCY'

As I write this book, my neighbour in the flat upstairs is stomping back and forth, making such a thumping racket that I'm finding it hard to concentrate and harder still to feel mercy! I complained to one of my friends about it and she encouraged me to see it as a wonderful opportunity to be merciful while I'm writing about mercy.

Gah!

When it is so hard to find mercy around or within us, perhaps it's no wonder that most of us struggle to believe God is as relentlessly merciful as the Bible says he is. Time and time again, I assume God is like me, or like the people around me, even though the Scriptures are absolutely clear that he is different, that his ways are not our ways and his thoughts are not our thoughts.

But it is not just when we look for mercy within and around us that we struggle. Sometimes it is the other attributes of God that cause us to doubt the extraordinariness of his mercy. Fallen humanity has a stubborn tendency to make God in our image, rather than to see him as he is. Our hearts fear that his love for us cannot possibly be as patient and kind, deep and wide, unending and unfailing as we are told.

So we raise objections to his mercy, wondering how it can possibly fit with his holiness, justice and anger. And if he is really as merciful as we are invited to believe, how do we square that with his discipline and our suffering?

When we make God in our own image, we can only see fractions of who he is, and even those are warped by our sin. Though I have walked with him for many years, I recognise how quickly my heart can still slip into seeing him as harsh, distant, cold, disappointed, frustrated and impatient.

I mess up and default to a posture of penance, as if I have forgotten that all the punishment for my sin has been placed on Jesus. Despite being told dozens of times in the Bible that God is slow to anger and abounding in steadfast love, despite reading page after page about his heart being moved to mercy towards all who turn to him, my heart is slow to believe and trust in it. It seems too good to be true. But the amazing reality is, when we see God as he really is, we don't have to suspend any parts of his character out of view. So, starting with the fact that mercy is not fair, we are going to look squarely in the face of the objections we raise to the mercy of God. Because when we look at him fully, we find that he is even more merciful than we dared to hope.

6

My unmerciful heart

Even though we are recipients of the mind-blowing mercy of God, we struggle to do as God says in Micah 6:8 and 'love mercy'. It is a great conundrum to me that I can be moved to tears of gratitude and joy by the mercy of God in my own life, yet sometimes find his mercy towards others offensive.

Though it baffles me, I know it is true: my heart simultaneously loves mercy and reacts against it. There are many reasons for this. The first is that it is not fair. This is such a big objection that the next chapter is devoted to it. The mercy of God is categorically unfair. Existing in a culture that is very much based on merit or rewards, my flawed heart can't quite get over the fact that my sin cannot put a dent in the ocean of God's mercy. I am delighted by this. But it is hard to have that same joy when I think about what other people have done. My sense of justice kicks in a lot faster than my sense of mercy.

I guess this is why Jesus had to remind the Pharisees that God desires mercy, not sacrifice, and accused them of shutting the kingdom of heaven in people's faces (Matthew 9:13, 23:13). Jesus says they have put heavy burdens on the people, while themselves neglecting the weightier matters of justice, mercy and faithfulness (Matthew 23:4, 23).

The Pharisees preferred a merit-based system of observing religious duties to earn the favour of God. And that would seem fairer to most of us. Except that there is no amount of religious duty we can observe that will earn our way into the favour and family of God, because we are fallen and sinful to such an absolute extent that even our good deeds are like filthy rags (Isaiah 64:6, NIV), stained as they are with the un-wash-out-able crimson oil of our sins (Isaiah 1:18).

Perhaps the Pharisees were unmerciful because they were more conscious of God's holiness, anger and discipline than they were of his love and kindness. Their name comes from the Hebrew for 'separate' or 'separated ones', and their focus was on strictly obeying God's laws. In many ways they sound like evangelical Christians today (like me), who can very quickly move from a God-honouring desire for holiness to a God-dishonouring legalism that quickly leads to a judgemental lack of mercy.

Many of us in the Western world perceive God as more harsh than merciful. We think of him as judge before we come to him as Father. Like Adam and Eve, we run from him when we have done wrong, adopting more of a 'my dad's going to kill me' posture, rather than running towards him like kids who have messed up and know they need their loving, reliable, protective Father to get them out of it.

We object to the mercy of God because we don't know him well enough. We see him through the lens of our culture, ourselves, or our earthly dads. We think that because we're quicker to judge than show mercy, he must be too. We also object to it because we want to contribute something to our standing with God. It is incomprehensible to us that we don't have to. Penance makes more sense, even to Protestants. But we cannot atone for our own sins and, wonderfully, because of the extraordinary mercy of God, we don't have to.

At the same time, we can also fall into thinking we are better than other people. Not all people, all of the time, but definitely some people, some of the time. I like reading about Peter in the Gospels because I can relate to him – I can easily imagine myself behaving like him: full of dedication to Jesus one minute and denying him the next; some days grasping the glory of who he is and other days totally missing the point of what he was saying.

While I can easily cast myself in Peter's role, I rarely think of myself as a Pharisee. They didn't follow Jesus, so I am not like them. I cannot relate to them. I think I am better than them.

And, in my estimation, I'm definitely better than abusers and rapists. I'm better than human traffickers and corrupt police officers. I'm better than COVID-deniers and those who partied during lockdowns. I'm better than people who fake illness or disability so they can get benefits they aren't entitled to. I'm better than people who think everyone on benefits is scrounging. I'm better than people who are promiscuous, who steal or who lie on their CVs. I'm better than dictators and parents who walk out on their kids. I'm better than people who don't say 'please' and 'thank you', and I'm better than the ungrateful and wicked. I'm also better than the Christians around me who don't understand the centrality of God's heart for those in poverty.

I get the irony that I sound just like the Pharisees Jesus rebuked for praying like this: 'God, I thank you that I am not like other men, extortioners, unjust, adulterers, or even like this tax collector' (Luke 18:11).

I am not proud of it. I am embarrassed by it. But if I'm honest with myself, I know that my heart, left to its own devices, is prone to placing people on a spectrum of good to bad, and to positioning myself towards the good end, the deserving end.

Whether we admit it or not, we all think we're better than other people, and this adds to our issues with loving mercy. There are so many people who don't deserve it. And even though I sometimes think it's too good to be true in my own life, I still feel as if my appeal to the mercy of God is stronger than other people's.

How terrifying and magnificent it is that God knows our hearts!

My righteousness

As I have mentioned, Jesus called out this exact thing when he told a parable 'to some who trusted in themselves that they were righteous, and treated others with contempt' (Luke 18:9). In it, he described those who thank God that they're not like other people and list the reasons why they are better.

I am frequently amazed at how often and how easily self-righteousness creeps into my heart. I find myself complaining to God about people in my life: 'God, she's so frustrating to work with because she just won't sit still and complete a task!' I could reel off countless examples of prayers I have prayed like that. But since I started writing this book (insert face-palm emoji!), God's response whenever I complain about someone is to say, gently, tenderly: 'You're like that, too.' And then he shows me the plank in my own eye. He doesn't hit me with it, but he humbles me with it. In doing so, he draws me back to his unmerited mercy towards me, and towards those around me.

When it comes to the mercy of God, we have problems with it when we look at God (*Isn't he holy and angry?*), at ourselves (*Surely it's too good to be true; it can't possibly be this easy*) and at others (*They don't deserve it*).

We also question whether or not it is wise. When you walk past someone begging on the street, how often has your first thought been: *If I give them money, I don't know what they will do with it*? Most of us would rather buy someone a sandwich. In fact, many of us would rather give nothing than risk the person spending our money on drugs or alcohol. We don't trust people to make good choices. More than that, we expect people – certain people, anyway – to make bad choices. Why would, or *should*, we be merciful to all, when some people cannot be trusted with our kindness?

It is worse still when someone has already blown a few chances. Have you seen this in church life, especially in our 'mercy ministries'? Someone is in need, so we help them out. We imagine that now we have helped them get back on their feet, they will stay there. But a few months later they ask for help a second time, because they're in need again. Maybe we help this time too, but we add some stronger guidance about how to make the most of what we are giving. What happens if they come back a third time? Surely we don't keep helping then.

I'm often asked to address this when I speak in churches about God's call on us to extend mercy in a way the world cannot. A lovely, dedicated servant of the Lord will come up to me after the service and explain a situation where it seems that someone is exploiting them. They will tell me how many chances they have given, how much help they have offered, and how weary, frustrated, upset, hurt or confused they are. We want to do good to others, but we also want to know when we can stop. But we're asking the wrong question.

It is perfectly valid and wise to ask *how* we should help someone, but God has already settled the matter of *if* we are to help the undeserving, ungrateful, ungodly or unwise. For God's people – his mercy-bringers – the question moves from 'Do I have to help you?' to 'What's the best way of helping you today?' It may not look like giving money to someone on the street, or continuing to offer the same support to someone who seems to be going in circles, but wisdom and mercy are not at odds. Far from it, actually, as James writes that wisdom from above is 'full of mercy' (James 3:17).

We will look more at the practical application of what it means to be merciful in Part 4, but for now let's take the time to work through some of our strongest objections to the mercy of God.

7

Mercy is not fair

My first job was serving ice creams on Hastings Pier. I was only thirteen, and my main task each weekend, as I saw it, was to serve the perfect Mr Whippy (soft serve for those reading outside the UK). I felt a great sense of pride if I got the curl of the pure white ice cream just right on the cone.

Sometimes I was transferred to the fudge shop, where I was mostly preoccupied with eating as many slivers of fudge as I could get away with, unnoticed. There was also a bingo hall where we served tea and coffee, and a burger bar right at the far end of the pier, which seemed so far out to sea to my little legs that it felt like being relegated to somewhere dim and distant.

The ice cream shop was my favourite place to work, and it was where most of us teenagers hoped to find ourselves stationed when we turned up on a Saturday morning. It was barely thirty years ago, but I was paid a minuscule amount by today's minimum wage standards at £1.32 per hour. My next job was at a local bridge club, serving tea and biscuits to elderly folk who met there three times a week to play cards. Though it was only two years later, I earned a whopping £5 per hour.

But I didn't feel hard done by when I was paid the lower amount. I could earn over £10 a day if I worked an eight-hour shift. To a thirteen-year-old in the days of penny sweets, this was wonderful. For the first few weeks of getting paid, I felt rich! I just wanted to earn my own money, so I didn't really care how much I was paid – I don't recall ever dwelling on the fact that my hourly pay on the pier was probably less than the cost of one of my perfectly produced ice creams.

It would have upset me, however, if there had been any unfairness in the pay structure. Even at that young age, I had an innate sense of wanting things to be fair. The way it worked on the pier was that your rate of pay was set by your age. So I didn't mind that the fifteen-year-olds got paid more than me, but I would have been furious if other thirteen-year-olds had been on a higher hourly rate.

Likewise, if I started at 10 a.m. and worked through to 6 p.m., I was really happy to take home the £10.56 I'd been promised. But imagine if someone who had started at 5 p.m. and finished at 6 p.m. had been given exactly the same amount at the end of the day. I would have been outraged. I would have kicked up a great fuss, protesting (rightly so!), 'That's not fair!'

So when I read the Parable of the Vineyard Owner in Matthew 20, I can relate to the disgruntled workers who laboured all day. Yes, they were paid what they had been promised. But still, wouldn't anyone be angry if those who worked for just one hour received the same pay?

God's mercy to us and those around us isn't fair, and that causes us problems.

I was reading Micah 6:8 a few years ago, perhaps for the hundredth time, and suddenly it leapt out at me. Why does God feel the need to tell his people to love mercy? What an odd thing for him to say to us. Obviously, I love mercy. I was saved by it.

So why does God tell us it is something he requires of us? Probably because he knows our tendency to receive his mercy for ourselves but resent it when it's shown to others.

An unmerciful prophet

Jonah is the classic example. This Old Testament prophet was tasked by God with taking a message of impending judgement to the people of Nineveh. But Jonah fled in the opposite direction and boarded a ship that would take him 'away from the presence of the LORD' (Jonah 1:3). However, God's people can't really run away from him. Jonah couldn't actually flee from his presence. God caused a great storm that threatened the safety of all on board. Their only salvation was in throwing the prophet overboard.

Jonah's disobedience could have cost his life and the lives of many others. Yet God, in his mercy, spared them all. In fact, he went to miraculous lengths to show mercy to Jonah. In one of the most fantastical stories in the Bible, God appointed a great fish to swallow him. As he languished inside the fish for three days, what must Jonah have been thinking? Maybe he spent a couple of days waiting to die, before finally grasping that God wanted to keep him alive.

We don't know how Jonah spent those three days, but we do know that there was a moment when he remembered God's mercy: 'I called out to the LORD, out of my distress, and he answered me… The waters closed in over me to take my life; the deep surrounded me; weeds were wrapped about my head… yet you brought up my life from the pit, O LORD my God' (Jonah 2:1-6). When Jonah remembered God's mercy and made vows to him, God commanded the fish to vomit Jonah onto the shore.

Not only did God spare Jonah's life, but his mercy extended further still, giving the prophet the same call on his life that he had received before he rebelled. So, having experienced mercy in such a remarkable way, Jonah did as God had asked – he went to Nineveh and delivered God's message. What followed is astonishing: unlike many pagan cities, the people of Nineveh believed what Jonah said and turned to God in repentance. Even the king called for everyone to repent and call out to God (Jonah 3).

What an incredible moment for the prophet Jonah. In theory.

I like to think that, had I been in Jonah's situation – sent on a mission by God that actually worked – I would be ecstatic. But while we might expect Jonah to be delighted at the impact his actions have on this great city, we instead find him 'exceedingly' displeased and so angry he wanted to die (Jonah 4:1-3).

Why?

Because this is why he ran away in the first place! He knew God would be merciful, and in this instance, he didn't want him to be. God's mercy made Jonah angry (Jonah 4:2).

Imagine receiving such astonishing mercy from God that the story would be told for centuries. Yet within forty days of your own miracle of mercy, you become so apoplectic with rage at God's mercy towards other people that you actually wish you were dead!

But we're nothing like Jonah… or are we? Remember, Jonah was a man of God. He was a Hebrew who believed in and feared the God of heaven and earth (Jonah 1:9). Yet if Jonah loved the mercy shown to him personally, but didn't love the mercy shown to others, it's *possible* that we might have a similar problem.

God delights in mercy. He loves it. If we're honest, *we* sometimes don't. Mercy isn't fair. Mercy is like the person who only worked for one hour being paid the same as the person who worked all day. Mercy is the people of Nineveh sinning wantonly and then repenting at the eleventh hour once God has given them the heads-up that destruction is coming.

Mercy is a gift, given freely, given liberally, given unfairly.

Receiving it is glorious, but loving it when it's shown to people we consider unworthy is hard. It's something we need to cultivate in our hearts, and that process can only start when we recognise how quickly we – just like Jonah – can become exceedingly annoyed by the unfairness of it.

8

But what about... the holiness of God?

I once joked with a friend that between us we had a very balanced view of God. She nicknamed me 'Mrs Mercy', and I was a little in awe of her laser focus on the holiness of God. Sometimes the combination seemed very complementary, but more often it felt like a glaring contrast.

It is easy to home in on the characteristics of God we like best. Contemplating his mercy is a joy for me, because I have grown to absolutely adore it. Once we start focusing on one attribute or another, we suddenly see it everywhere. As we read the Scriptures, verses come alive to us that help us grasp it more keenly. Having spent the last few years doing a 'deep dive' into the mercy of God, it is now my natural inclination when I think of him to dwell on the truth that he is merciful.

Once we have established such a precious and profound understanding of one element of God's nature, it can have the unintended consequence that we neglect other aspects of who God is and develop a lopsided view of him. Perhaps you're thinking that about me after reading Part 1's chapters on the rich, unrestrained, relentless mercy of God! As I delight in the mercy of God that has dealt with all my sins, maybe you're thinking: *OK, I get it, but what about...?* And possibly the first 'what about?' that comes to mind is 'what about the holiness of God?'

The apostle Paul anticipated a similar question in his letter to the Church in Rome. After stressing that salvation is a free gift from God, and hammering home the point that 'where sin increased, grace abounded all the more' (Romans 5:20), he then heads off the key objection at the pass, writing: 'What shall we say then? Are we to continue in sin that grace may abound? By no means!' (Romans 6:1–2).

Just as the grace of God reveals our sinfulness and also empowers us to say no to sin, so the mercy of God helps us to find the holiness of God all the more beautiful, while the holiness of God shines a powerful spotlight on just how incredible his mercy is.

We are not supposed to separate the attributes of God – they can't be separated. They are wonderfully interwoven, and when we start to comprehend that, we find God more glorious than ever.

God is holy. That means he is perfect in all his ways. He never does anything wrong. He never has skewed thinking. He never lies. He never changes. He is totally pure, totally righteous, totally good. His holiness is beautiful.

Always good, always true

For one thing, it means we can trust him completely. He never has a bad day. He doesn't have a dark side. He is not prone to losing his temper or changing his ways.

The greatest pain I have experienced in relationships always comes down to people (including me) not being trustworthy – either not being who they said they were, or not keeping promises they made, or both. Our deepest hurts are often caused by failed expectations, changes in affection or broken promises.

I have found that there is nothing like the grief of being let down by someone (or letting someone down myself) to drive me deeper into gratitude that God is not like us. He never fails us, never forsakes us, never turns his back on us. We can depend on him without fear, because he is good all the time, and his mercies and steadfast love endure forever.

Because he is holy, he cannot lie. 'Jesus Christ is the same yesterday and today and forever' (Hebrews 13:8). 'There is nothing deceitful in God, nothing two-faced, nothing fickle' (James 1:17, MSG). God 'does not change like shifting shadows' (James 1:17, NIV).

This is a wonderful truth that brings us great security. Because God is holy, we have no need to fear that one day we will wake up and he will be different. We can trust that he will always do what is right. *Always*. He will never do anything sinful or evil or wicked or bad. Everything he does is good, pleasing, perfect and righteous. He doesn't veer even one millimetre off course from his complete holiness.

Reflecting on the holiness of God makes his mercy more beautiful than it was before, because it shows us two things. The first is just how sinful we are; how unlike him we are. My thoughts and actions are tainted with mixed motives, at best. All have the thread of sin woven into them. Sometimes this is really obvious – when we do 'big things' wrong – other times it's far more subtle. But the more we gaze on the holiness of God, the more we see our own sinfulness, our own brokenness, and how flawed we are.

The second thing the holiness of God shows us is that his mercy is all the more surprising – utterly outrageous, even – because this holy, perfect God, who never does anything wrong, draws me in as his beloved daughter. I shouldn't be able to come anywhere near God. Yet, by his astonishing mercy, I can come freely, boldly, confidently into the presence of our holy God. He knows my sin. Not one tiny bit is hidden from him. But because he is merciful, he has made a way, through the cross of Christ, for me to find his holiness beautiful and to reverently revel and rejoice in it, rather than cower and take cover.

Far from causing us to be ambivalent about the sin in our lives, the merciful kindness of God draws us to pursue holiness. Even when we wander, God never drags us back kicking and screaming – he leads us with 'cords of kindness, with the bands of love' (Hosea 11:4), and heals our apostasy and waywardness (Hosea 14:4).

God's holiness and mercy are not at war. Whenever we think or act as if they are, we have strayed from seeing God as he really is. He is fully merciful and completely holy. His holiness shows me that I need his mercy, and his mercy makes me want to be holy.

It is as we focus our gaze on his incomprehensibly beautiful mercy at work in our lives that we find the desire welling up within us to love, adore, obey, honour, worship and serve him with every fibre of our being, living holy lives that are pleasing in his sight.

9

But what about... the justice of God?

When twenty-four-year-old Nikolas Cruz, the gunman who mercilessly killed seventeen people at Parkland School in Florida, was sentenced to life in prison instead of being executed, the victims' families were outraged. 'I feel angry. I feel rage. I feel that justice wasn't served,' said one mum whose teenage son was murdered in the shooting.[1]

In November 2022, Cruz was given thirty-four life sentences without the possibility of parole for killing these seventeen people and attempting to kill a further seventeen. It was widely expected that he would be given the death penalty. He was described by one woman who lost her sister in the high school shooting as 'a remorseless monster who deserves no mercy'.[2]

Another woman, who lost her fourteen-year-old granddaughter in the massacre, addressed Cruz with the words: 'I hope your every breathing moment here on Earth is miserable and you repent for your sins, Nikolas, and burn in hell.'[3]

Fred Guttenberg, whose daughter was killed, said: 'In prison I hope and pray he receives the kind of mercy from prisoners that he showed to my daughter and the 16 others.'[4]

Such gut-wrenching, heartbreaking grief demands justice. We may not have experienced such a brutal loss, but the families' desire for justice is likely to resonate with us.

Perhaps one of the toughest challenges of the Christian faith is trying to reconcile the God-given – and God-like – desire for justice with a love for mercy. Outside the cross of Christ, can justice and mercy co-exist? Is it even possible?

Justice and mercy are placed side by side throughout the Bible. When Micah told us to love mercy, he also told us to 'act justly' (Micah 6:8, NIV). Justice and mercy cannot be incompatible, since God not only encourages us to do both, but actually *requires* us to do both. He does not give us freedom to choose one over the other. But how do we begin to do both?

Perfect justice

First of all, it's vital to know that the Lord is 'a God merciful' *and* 'a God of justice' (Isaiah 30:18). Justice is just as much a part of his character as mercy. Scripture after Scripture proclaims it, leaving us no room for doubt that God is just and cares vehemently about justice.

'*He is* the Rock, His work *is* perfect; For **all His ways *are* justice**, a God of truth and without injustice; righteous and upright *is* He' (Deuteronomy 32:4, NKJV, bold added).

All his ways are justice. There is no injustice in him.

When God revealed himself to Moses as 'a God merciful', he also promised he would 'by no means clear the guilty' (Exodus 34:7).

Our innate sense of justice – the inbuilt sense of what is right and wrong, and that there should be punishment or atonement for wrongdoing – comes from God. It is one of the ways in which we are made in his image. We reflect his nature, which explains why kindness is valued across the world and murder is considered wrong in every nation.[5] God has designed us to be aggrieved by injustice.

We react against injustice even in the most minor of matters: someone pushes in front of us in a queue; the driver who hit our car gets away with it; a colleague we consider lazy gets a performance-related pay rise, but we don't.

We all want justice when we are harmed in some way – that is a normal human reaction – but our sense of justice and injustice is imperfect. The reality for me is that I want justice when I'm wronged, but mercy when I am in the wrong. My *standard* of justice goes up and down; it is inconsistent. Likewise, my *desire* for justice fluctuates according to the situation. We plead the case of those we love even when they are clearly at fault, but will not accept any excuses when someone we do not like hurts someone we love.

I have done this myself when it comes to people I know who have had extramarital affairs. When others have condemned a friend who cheated, I have rushed to present mitigating circumstances, to give the other side of the story. But at the same time, when it comes to my friends being cheated on, I have found myself arguing, hypocritically: 'There is no excuse!'

We see this play out in celebrity culture, where some people seem to be beyond accountability for their actions. It baffles me that some celebrities seem to get away with making racist remarks, perpetrating domestic violence or even abusing children, just because they are a national treasure or musical genius, yet others are vilified and considered beyond redemption.

What's the difference? There isn't one, but our sense of justice is not impartial. It depends a lot on whom we are talking about and the circumstances of their wrongdoing, as we understand or interpret them.

My sense of justice is volatile, and influenced by many factors.

Thankfully – mercifully – God is not like me. He is not like us. He is perfectly just. *All* his ways are just. His justice is proportionate, measured and balanced. He is not harsh on his enemies and lenient towards his friends. As the repeated New Testament use of the Greek word *prosôpolêptês* (and variants of it) tells us, God is no respecter of persons. He shows no partiality when it comes to his standards of justice.[6] He acts with equity and fairness towards all.

And because he is God, he knows the whole story about every situation. He is fully aware of the facts. He has seen and heard everyone's version of events. He doesn't only know what happened; he is also aware of the motives behind it. He knows our hearts.

Interestingly, I cannot find any example in the Bible where God puts forward mitigating circumstances for someone's sin. He knows why we do the things we do – he is acquainted with all our ways (Psalm 139:3) – but he does not give us excuses that let us off the hook when it comes to sin and justice. The only reason any of us can receive God's mercy is that his justice was satisfied through the death of Jesus on the cross in our place. We do not receive his mercy at the expense of his justice. We receive both. The punishment we deserve has not been swept away. It has been given to Jesus, who bore our sins (Isaiah 53).

Wonderfully, God promises that one day there will be perfect justice. This can provide great comfort for any of us living with ongoing injustice in our lives. When Jesus returns and the kingdom of God is rolled out in full, there will be complete justice. Every wrong will be made right.

The wait for certain, perfect justice empowers us to love mercy today.

Justice and mercy

One of the things that is distinctive about the Christian faith is that the God of the Bible doesn't do away with justice so he can offer us mercy. Satisfying justice and delightful mercy co-exist in perfect harmony. Justice was delivered in full when Jesus died on the cross to take the punishment for our sins, and mercy is available to anyone who humbly asks for it.

Followers of Jesus are not to choose mercy over justice or justice over mercy. We are to act justly *and* love mercy. We have an example of this in Mary's husband, Joseph. We don't know much about him, other than that he was 'a just man' who was somehow able to combine justice with mercy in the way he planned to treat Mary. Until he was told by an angel to go ahead with the marriage, his *just* character led him to be *mercifully* 'unwilling to put her to shame' (Matthew 1:19–25).

Biblical justice leaves space for mercy. Its ultimate desire is not retribution, but repentance, which means it doesn't rule out redemption (Ezekiel 18:23). Followers of Jesus are to act justly, work for wrong things to be made right, speak up against injustice and pray that God will 'let justice roll down like waters' (Amos 5:24). But at the same time we are to cultivate a love for mercy in our hearts that longs for repentance that can lead to rehabilitation, redemption and restoration, where possible.

God is not passive about justice and injustice. Just as he delights in mercy, so he delights in justice (Jeremiah 9:24, NIV). When Jesus rebukes the Pharisees for neglecting the weightier matters of the law, he names mercy *and* justice.

The beautiful truth is not that we get mercy without justice, nor justice without mercy, but both, perfectly entwined. God is abundantly merciful and entirely just.

10

But what about... the anger of God?

My most controversial social media post was when I tweeted something defending the American pastor and preacher Tim Keller for saying it is good that God gets angry. I was amazed at the vitriol my tweet attracted. I struggled to understand why people were so upset about the idea that God gets angry, because I am relieved that he does. God is provoked to anger, and God is merciful. These two facts are not at odds.

Anger is a difficult subject, which is probably why we don't hear much about it. Like many of the upset tweeters, I tend to consider it as a negative thing when I think about it in abstract terms. The examples that spring to mind tend to be connected to bad human anger – anger that is unwarranted, disproportionate, unpredictable or abusive.

The way we think and feel about anger will depend on our personal experiences of it. Some of us have been scarred by someone else's unrestrained anger, which may have expressed itself in brutal words etched into our memories, affecting how we think about ourselves, or in violence. Some of us have physical and psychological scars from the anger of others. Some of us are ashamed that we struggle to control our temper. Some of us know that we get irrationally angry; others of us won't let ourselves feel anger at all.

But not all anger is sinful. Much the opposite. There is an anger that is right, good and wholly appropriate. In fact, sometimes *failing* to be angry is to have missed the heart of God – sometimes a lack of anger is actually sin. It is often the case that those of us living in relative comfort in the wealthiest nations are the ones who most struggle with the anger of God, while people living in situations where injustice is an ever-present reality, such as conflict zones, are more likely to feel that God is not angry enough.

Righteous anger

When appropriate, anger is a godly response. I'm not talking about the trivial things that make us angry, but the traumatic. There are several minor grievances, petty in the grand scheme of things, that wind me up. Here are just a few.

People driving really slowly, especially when I'm in a hurry. (Honestly, sometimes I think I'm at my absolute worst when driving behind someone who is doing 30mph when the speed limit is 60mph!)

When people don't say thank you when I hold a door open for them.

Being put on hold for ages or receiving a cold call. Some days that's enough to make me angry.

But there are much more serious things that make me angry, too. Things that strike at the very heart of who we are, and of God's design and intention for us.

In April 2018, I visited Cambodia with International Justice Mission (IJM) to see its work rescuing victims and supporting survivors of human trafficking. In a modest church in a rural village near Siem Reap, I listened with horror as two men shared their experiences of being modern-day slaves. Both had been lured into the Thai fishing industry with promises of lucrative pay. Both had travelled across the border in good faith, wanting to provide for their families. Both were then enslaved.

One of these men hadn't seen land for six years. He was transferred from boat to boat, without sanitation or bedding.

Within his first few days, he witnessed the captain slit another slave's throat – a brutal warning of what would happen if he caused any trouble. During shifts that lasted two nights and three days, he was beaten with metal rods if he fell asleep. He had accepted the job with joy, believing it would pay for his kids' education. Instead, he had no way of contacting them or his wife for more than six years. They thought he was dead. He also thought he would die.

Hearing his story, I was flooded with emotion. Mostly, I was horrified and troubled, and felt compassion for the man and his family. But I also felt outraged that people could do such a barbaric thing to a fellow human being. I was angry, and it is absolutely right that this made me angry. This was righteous anger.

I felt the same way when I visited Cape Coast Castle in Ghana and learned about white Christians living in luxury and singing hymns loudly to drown out the sounds of the suffering African slaves who were imprisoned in underground dungeons beneath them before being transported against their will to be sold in America or Europe. It is right to be angry about historic slavery and modern-day slavery. God is angry about both (Ezekiel 22:29–30).

The kind of slavery I heard about in Cambodia doesn't just happen in far-flung corners of the world. Around the time of my trip, I was working with local police in my home town of Hastings, on the south-east coast of England, to raise awareness about human trafficking and modern slavery. As chair of the Hastings Anti-Trafficking Hub, I was well aware that slavery is a reality in communities across the UK, including my own. But I had no idea how close to home it actually was until, just a couple of weeks after returning from Cambodia, I chaperoned some local journalists on a police raid to rescue victims, only to discover that I didn't need to fly 6,000 miles across the world to meet victims of slavery – I could have walked 60 yards to the end of my street, where it transpired that a house just a few doors down from my flat was 'home' to almost a dozen victims of labour trafficking.

Again, I felt numerous emotions in response to this: shock, confusion and indignation. Anger was, once again, absolutely the right response to such injustice and brutality.

Slow to anger

It is right that we allow ourselves to feel anger at injustice, even actively working to cultivate it where we lack a holy anger about the things that anger God. But it is vital that we let that anger and outrage propel us into speaking up for those who cannot speak for themselves (Proverbs 31:8–9), and demonstrating the mercy and justice of God, and not into fits of rage, unkind words or vigilante revenge. God's anger is not like that.

It is also worth remembering that our human anger can be very selective. There are atrocities that happen all over the world that do not cause me the same degree of anger that I feel about slavery. And even when I am rightly angry, I struggle to find any space for mercy.

Thankfully, God doesn't.

God is angry about abuse, oppression, racism, exploitation, murder, profiting at the expense of others and tearing down someone's character with lies. It's good that God is angry about these things. It is holy. It is just. It is right. I'm glad God gets angry. But I'm also incredibly grateful that his anger makes way for his mercy – that his 'mercy triumphs over judgement' (James 2:13).

Dane Ortlund points out in *Gentle and Lowly* that we tend to think God is quick to anger and slow to show mercy, but it's the opposite. God is quick to show mercy but has to be extensively provoked to anger.[1] Even when provoked, he warns us of impending judgement – that's exactly what happened with Jonah and the Ninevites. God sent Jonah to tell them their evil was about to be punished but, even in his wrath, God remembered mercy (Habakkuk 3:2). And when the people of Nineveh repented, the Lord relented. God's anger is measured and held back; his mercy is abundant and unrestrained.

Our anger can be like a volcano, bottled up and then unleashed, devastating everything nearby. God's anger is completely different. His anger is always righteous. We don't have to wonder from one day to the next what makes him angry, or whether he's in an angry mood. His anger is not like ours. God doesn't lose his temper. He doesn't have fits of uncontrollable rage.

We see this with Jesus. In John's Gospel, we read that when Jesus got angry and cleared the temple of money-changers, it wasn't in a fit of rage but was planned. He had seen what was happening in the temple and *made a whip of cords* to drive them out (John 2:15). He took the time to make it. It was considered.

Not only is God slow to anger, but his anger is consistent, measured and proportionate. Therefore, we can trust it. We can trust him.

Because we can trust the anger of God, we can forgive others and not take revenge. We too can be slow to anger, just as God commands us to be in James 1, because we can entrust our anger at injustice – at wrongs that have been done to us and to others – to God.

This doesn't mean we should not be angry. But it does mean we can pursue mercy as we reflect on the amazing truth of the gospel that God's anger – his appropriate, measured, righteous anger towards us for the things we've done wrong, for the harm we've caused to other people – and the punishment we deserved, have been poured out on Jesus in our place.

We have provoked God to anger, and we have been shown mercy. By placing our trust in Jesus, we have been forgiven. Not only that, but we have also been cleansed of our unrighteousness (1 John 1:9) and need never fear the anger of God because on the 'day of vengeance of our God' (Isaiah 61:2) we can plead the cross of Jesus in our defence. On that day, when God's anger is poured out on sin and all injustice is put right, we will see our own sin as it really is – every evil deed, every wicked thought, vast in volume, unspeakable in nature, overwhelming in its unhidden awfulness – and we will know, in that very same moment, that the blood of Jesus has covered us completely.

What astonishing mercy!

11
But what about... the discipline of God?

The beautiful British city of Canterbury offers punting tours along the river, where you can enjoy the history and scenery in tranquillity as you glide along the water. In theory. That is not quite how I experienced it the day I got into one of the boats with friends and their two small children! While their three-year-old repeatedly tried to lean over the side to sneakily drink some of the green river water, hoping not to be caught by his dad, their eighteen-month-old screamed incessantly for almost the entire forty-five minutes. She wriggled, writhed, pushed and kicked, desperately trying to free herself from her mum's arms, because she wanted to be in the water.

Of course, all the adults on board knew that if she got into the water, it wouldn't be the fun she expected it to be, and could even be life-threatening – best-case scenario, she swallows some water and is sick; worst-case scenario, she drowns. But this precious little toddler had no idea of the danger she would be in. All she saw was water, and she wanted in! The more she struggled, the more her mum tightened her grip. The toddler never tired of fighting, not in three-quarters of an hour. There was no persuading her that her mum's refusal to let her into the water was for her own good. At eighteen months that's no surprise... but as an adult, what's my excuse?

I ask that question because it wasn't long after this trip that I felt God remind me of this incident and point out that I am often just like my friend's daughter. I haven't kept count of my battles with God, but I know there have been many, many times in my life when I have, in a spiritual sense, wriggled, writhed and screamed, fighting God, kicking against what he is trying to do in my life, or arguing repeatedly for something I want that he won't give me.

I want my way, and I wrestle with God to get it. All I can see is the water, which looks so fun and inviting. I forget that he knows better than I do what is good for me and what is harmful. So I struggle like a one-year-old, trying to get my way, trying to release his firm hold on me or my circumstances and often completely failing to understand that it is his mercy towards me that causes him to keep that tight grip on me.

Tracing his hand

When we start to really delve deep into the mercies of God, meditating on the fact that they are new every morning, we slowly begin to grasp that everything that happens to us – everything God allows to take place in our lives – is a mercy to us, or can be transformed into one, by his grace. This is hard for us to believe. It certainly feels like a 'slippery' truth to me, like trying to hold water in my hands. I get it. I see it. It's there. Then it's gone. Nevertheless, it's the truth. However hard it is to hold on to, however difficult it is to see and believe it in the difficult seasons of life, the fact remains that God is abundantly merciful. No matter how hard my friend's daughter fought, no matter how loudly she yelled, there was no way her mum would have given in and let her child throw herself into the water. Likewise, even when we fight against our Father in heaven, he won't give in and give us what we want when he knows full well that it will do us harm.

When I'm wrestling with God like this, holding on to the truth that he is merciful is the hardest part. I drift – or sometimes even throw myself – into thinking he is mean. Like an eighteen-month-old, I cannot understand why God is holding me so tight, not letting me go where I want, have what I want, do what I want.

But I struggle because I don't understand. I cannot see the whole picture. God is the One who knows the end from the beginning (Isaiah 46:9–10). I don't. I can't.

So that's when knowing and trusting his merciful heart becomes all the more important. As Spurgeon put it, God is 'too wise to err and too good to be unkind',[1] and that is why we can trust him. Another quote attributed to Spurgeon is: 'When you cannot trace his hand, you can trust his heart.' But I find it can be harder to trust God when you *do* trace his hand. When you believe he is at work, either causing or permitting a bad thing, or withholding a seemingly good thing – it can be harder to hold on to an unshakeable belief in his merciful heart.

The Bible doesn't shy away from this. There are plenty of times when a psalmist or prophet states plainly that they believe God has caused the circumstances that are distressing them (for example, Psalms 60:3, 71:20, 118:18, 119:75; Lamentations 2; Hosea 6:1). Like David, Job and Jeremiah, I find the hardest thing to do when I am lamenting my troubles is not to hold on to the fact that God is merciful when I cannot trace his hand, but to do so when I can clearly see his hand at work in what is happening to me.

This is where the rubber hits the road, and the certainty of our belief that God is merciful is most tested. Looking back over my trials, disappointments, suffering and wrestling, can I say, like Hezekiah, 'It was for my welfare that I had great bitterness [or anguish]' (Isaiah 38:17)? Better still, can I learn from past experiences to hold firm to this in the present, when I am distressed and baffled as to where the new mercy of God is for this day?

I am not trying to get into a theological debate here about whether the bad things that happen to us are caused by God or simply permitted by him, or even happen outside of his will and are subsequently redeemed by him. I lean towards one of these viewpoints more than the others, but it is a mystery – and no one can be certain of the answer because God has not explicitly told us. But what I do know for certain is that the Father is at work in everything that happens in our lives, and his work is always merciful, and always for our good and his glory.

Refined by fire

The Bible tells us we have been called by God and predestined by him for a specific purpose, and that purpose is 'to be conformed to the image of his Son' (Romans 8:29).

In the Western world, we often hear a distorted but more palatable version of the gospel, which is along the lines of: 'Come to Jesus and he will make your life better.' That is true, of course, but not in the way our modern ears may interpret it. The testimonies we showcase from our platforms often present Christianity as the answer to all our troubles – for example, 'I was sick and now I'm healed' or 'I was addicted and now I'm free' or 'I was a criminal and now I'm a responsible citizen' or 'I was depressed and now I'm full of joy'. Stories like these are wonderful. God is a miracle-working God who sometimes intervenes supernaturally and instantaneously in our lives in these kinds of ways. But it's not the whole story, and it's not the whole gospel.

Jesus clearly stated that we would have trouble. We can be certain of it. But when we go through troubled times, God refines us in the midst of them. Whether or not the trouble comes from him, whether or not it comes to us with his permission – whatever you believe about that – God is at work in every hard season, redeeming even the most painful of circumstances by working all things together for our good through them. He is committed to purifying and sanctifying us, making us more like Jesus, if we will let him mould and discipline us. He is more concerned about our hearts than our comfort, but he is also so incredibly merciful that he takes our sins and mistakes, and turns them for our good (Romans 8:28).

My knee-jerk reaction to anything I feel is the discipline of God in my life is to kick against it: to wrestle, or even rebel. I find it hard to shake my deep-rooted impression that discipline is bad. But in Proverbs we're instructed not to despise God's discipline, and not to be weary, upset, grieved or resentful when he corrects us (Proverbs 3:11). Why should we embrace God's discipline? Because it's a sign of his love for, and delight in, us (Proverbs 3:12). He disciplines us in his mercy. He is not about making people nice or improving our lives with his blessings. His vision for us extends far beyond that. We are being completely transformed, redeemed, remade to be more like Jesus.

Sometimes the path to maturity is painful. Sometimes it feels as if we are being held by God in the fiery furnace until we are refined (Isaiah 48:9–10). That can be confusing, when we know him as the tender and compassionate One. But it is because of his mercy that he is refining and purifying us to make us more like Jesus – the very purpose for which we were predestined, called and chosen.

God is not like a genie, who grants us three wishes and then does whatever we ask. And he is not like Santa Claus, who keeps a record of how we behave and then grants us gifts if we are good, but withholds them if we are naughty. No. Much more wonderfully, he is our merciful Father, who loves us too much to let us have our way when he knows it will harm us or those around us. This means that sometimes we might feel, as Job, David and Hezekiah did at various points, that it is God who is afflicting us. But when we look for God's mercy, even as he disciplines us, we will find, like Job, that we can proclaim: 'Behold, blessed is the one whom God reproves; therefore despise not the discipline of the Almighty. For he wounds, but he binds up; he shatters, but his hands heal' (Job 5:17–18).

12

But what about... my suffering?

I went through a period of about six or seven years when it felt like one painful thing happened after another. It didn't feel like a season of distress; it felt as if I had taken up permanent residence in the valley of the shadow of death. Every time I tried to get to higher ground, I slid back down.

In fact, midway through what already felt like a prolonged period of pain, I was on a leadership training course where the church leader who was speaking told stories about everything he had been through in recent years. He said he had reached a point where he felt that one more thing would break him, and then he invited any of us who felt like that to stand so we could receive prayer. It felt as if he was speaking just to me, so I stood. I was battle-weary, overwhelmed with sorrow, fearful of the future, and felt there was no way I could face another horrible thing happening to me or someone close to me.

A few friends from my church gathered around me. As they prayed, I experienced the presence of God and felt as if a line had been drawn in the sand. I thought that was that – no more bad things would happen for a long time – and I felt thoroughly relieved.

Less than thirty hours later, I was serving on the audio-visual team for my church's Sunday evening meeting when I received a text. It was from the father of my closest friend from sixth-form college, Sophie. I don't remember exactly what the message said, but it was something simple, like: 'Natalie, I'm Sophie's dad. Please would you call me?' I had not seen him for several years, so I knew that hearing from him out of the blue was unlikely to be good news.

I was right. When I called the number he had given, I spoke with Sophie's mum, and she told me that Sophie had died. I knew she'd had cancer a few years earlier, but I didn't know she had been suffering with it again. She hadn't told any of her old school friends. I had tried to contact her a few times in the previous few months and wondered why she hadn't replied, but as we weren't in regular contact I hadn't dwelt on it too much.

About six months before she died, I was travelling with work and realised I was really close to where she lived. I thought about calling in on the off-chance she was free for a drink, but instead I decided to get on the road. Hearing that Sophie had died, I desperately wished we'd had a chance to talk in her last few months. I was instantly swamped with regret. And I was furious with God! I wasn't just angry because my friend had died at the age of thirty-seven, as tragic as that was. It wasn't that I simply blamed him for letting me drive away just a few months earlier or felt upset that he hadn't prompted me to be more persistent in trying to contact her. *Why didn't he tell me?* It was also because the news of Sophie's death came in the context of my responding for prayer the day before and categorically letting God know that one more thing would break me. Hadn't he understood that we – he and I together, I'd thought – had developed an understanding about my capacity for upsetting news, and had drawn a line the very day before? I didn't just feel sadness, grief and anger. I was deeply confused.

The next day, I told a friend I wasn't going to speak in churches or write on poverty any more, because every time I did, something horrible happened. I had started to associate these continual heartaches with my increasing opportunities to speak and write about God's mercy towards the most vulnerable. When Sophie died, I thought: *That's it. I can't do it any more. It's too hard and it's too painful.* I was upset, and I'd been upset about one thing or another for most of the previous three years.

Where's the power?

When we are suffering, it can feel like rubbing salt in the wound to say: 'God is still merciful, even in this.' If we try hard and really fix our eyes on Jesus, we may be able to say that God is still good, no matter what. But how can his mercy be at work in my life daily, when each day brings fresh sadness and hurt?

This is a question I have asked myself time and time again. In times of suffering, it is so hard to see clearly who God is, and how he interacts with us. I have spent much of my life battling a crippling fear of rejection and abandonment. It has affected my relationships, friendships, work and pretty much every area of my life. I reached a point during this prolonged period of suffering where I gave up hope that I would ever be free of this fear. Each thing that happened seemed to compound it and cause it to grow.

I wrestled with God over it. I would quote his words at him, saying: 'The Bible says the same power that raised Jesus from the dead is at work in me. So where is it, Father?' I was having counselling to help me understand why I carried these persistent fears that I could not shake, which were damaging every area of my life and making me miserable, as well as affecting several people around me. I told my counsellor I had reached a place of resignation, believing the words 'rejection' and 'abandonment' would always speak a louder word over me than the name of Jesus.

In the midst of this season, a friend from another church prophesied over me that God had called me to be someone who proclaims: 'Change is possible.' As she spoke these words over me, I responded in my head with desperate sadness: 'I can't, God. I don't believe it.' I had lost confidence that the gospel had the power to bring deep, lasting, fundamental change. I looked at the pain and sadness around me, at friends who had suffered or struggled with persistent situations or issues, and concluded that the power of the gospel is not available in this life, but will be a reality only when we see Jesus face to face.

To my amazement, it turned out I was wrong. Six years into this season of suffering, where lifelong issues seemed to be dragged to the surface with every passing trauma or sad event, breakthrough came. There wasn't a 'magic' moment. I didn't find a mighty man or woman of God to lay hands on me and have my problems disappear immediately (though this can happen). It didn't happen in an instant, but suddenly I started to see chinks of light, glimmers of hope, as pennies started dropping in my thought processes. What followed was an incredible few months of joy as my thinking changed, my fears receded, and my security grew and grew.

Life settled down to 'normal', but a fundamental change had taken place in me. I noticed I reacted differently to things that would, in the past, have sent me into a spiral of perceived rejection and subsequent depression. Instead of being hypervigilant for signs of rejection (my counsellor once observed that if there was the slightest iota of rejection a thousand miles away, I would spot it), I became hypervigilant for signs of God's mercy at work in my life. In fact, I messaged one of my friends so often to tell her every small mercy I noticed, she said I could stop now if I wanted to! (She quickly changed her mind and came back, saying: 'Actually, please keep telling me.')

With each tiny change I observed, I felt deep joy and wonder. I really started to identify with the people around Jesus who 'disbelieved for joy' (Luke 24:41) and were 'astonished beyond measure' (Mark 7:37) as I, too, could barely believe how the power of the gospel was transforming my thinking from my lifelong beliefs about myself, other people and God. I realised how my past suffering had led me to this point. To my great shock, I found myself feeling grateful for God's mercy in letting me go through things that had subsequently resulted in my freedom and joy.

The thing I greatly feared

But then, after two years of experiencing such wonderful changes, something happened that completely floored me. Having spent decades fearing rejection and abandonment that were mostly in my head, I experienced them for real. I called my counsellor and said, through sobs: 'You equipped me to deal with this when it was all in my imagination, but I don't know how to deal with it now that it's actually happening.'

What made this suffering harder to bear was that it was all the more traumatic because of how far I'd come. When I lived in constant fear of rejection and abandonment, I kept my guard up. I protected myself. But because of God's powerful, transformative work in my life, I no longer operated like that. I felt safe. I felt secure. So I was completely blindsided when rejection and abandonment happened for real. The shock was one of the factors that made it so painful.

I found comfort in the words of Job: 'For the thing I greatly feared has come upon me, and what I dreaded has happened to me. I am not at ease, nor am I quiet; I have no rest, for trouble comes' (Job 3:25–26, NKJV). It helped to know that Job had felt the same way, that the very thing he greatly feared had happened to him, too. I struggled for months to see God's mercy at work in this new suffering. But I kept asking him to reveal it, because I knew it must be there, even if it was hidden from my sight by the pain I was in. Like Job, I kept praying: 'But as for me, I would seek God, and to God I would commit my cause – who does great things, and unsearchable, marvelous things without number' (Job 5:8–9, NKJV).

And now, with hindsight, I once again see the mercy of God through my trials, through my suffering. I could fill a whole chapter describing how experiencing the very thing I dreaded has transformed me in ways I could not have imagined possible. It brought me closer to Jesus than ever before. It was worth it, because through it I experienced an intimacy and consistency in my walk with him that I had never known before. What felt like a brutal pummelling has resulted in precious truths being kneaded deeper into my heart. I now know that I am Christ's beloved in such a beautifully profound way, and this has brought a steadiness and stability to my emotions and my life that I had never known before.

Though I couldn't see it at the time, and can rarely see it clearly while in the middle of it, even these painful seasons have proved to be God's kind-hearted mercy towards me, drawing me close, enveloping me in his love, and whispering gently but powerfully to the depths of my heart. I would not undo the trials I have been through, excruciatingly painful as some of them were.

Even in my suffering – perhaps especially there – God's tender mercies have been new every morning.

13

Mercy in the wilderness

Many of the people in the Bible who were closest to God went through wilderness seasons – times when they were separated from those around them and, in some cases, felt as if God were nowhere to be found. Often they were there because other people had mistreated them, but sometimes they were there because of their own sin. Either way, we repeatedly see in Scripture that God is just as much the God of the wilderness as he is the God of the mountains.

If mountaintop experiences tend to reveal God in powerful and glorious ways – think Moses, Elijah and Jesus' transfiguration, for example – there seems to be an intimacy and tenderness when God comes to people in the rough, dry wilderness places.

It was in the wilderness that God came to Hagar – twice (Genesis 16:7–14, 21:14–21) – and it was there that she encountered him as the God who sees us in our distress and looks after us (Genesis 16:13). It was in the wilderness that God appeared to Moses through a burning bush to tell him he had seen the affliction of his people and would rescue them from their oppression (Exodus 3:1–10).

When God set his people free from Pharaoh and the Egyptians, he 'did not lead them by the way... that was near... But God led the people round by the way of the wilderness towards the Red Sea' (Exodus 13:17–18). It was in the wilderness that God performed extraordinary miracles – parting the waters before them, appearing as a pillar of cloud and a pillar of fire, turning water from bitter to sweet, providing bread from heaven every day for four decades, and more.

The wilderness was where the Israelites discovered God's loving tenderness towards them: 'The LORD your God carried you, as a man carries his son' (Deuteronomy 1:31) and: 'He found him in a desert land, and in the howling waste of the wilderness; he encircled him, he cared for him, he kept him as the apple of his eye' (Deuteronomy 32:10).

It was in the wilderness that the shepherd-boy David learned to walk closely with God (1 Samuel 17:28), and it was in various wilderness places that David-the-anointed-king knew the protection of God from his enemies (1 Samuel 23:14–25).

It was in the wilderness that an angel sent by God gave Elijah food, water and rest when he wanted to die (1 Kings 19:2–8). It was in the wilderness that John the Baptist preached a message of repentance and the forgiveness of sins, preparing the way for Jesus (Mark 1:3–4).

Jesus himself was led into the wilderness by the Holy Spirit to be tempted by the devil (Matthew 4:1), emerging forty days later in the power of the Spirit to start his public ministry (Luke 4:14). It was to the wilderness that he later returned to avoid those who wanted to kill him (John 11:53–54), and that he frequently withdrew to pray to his Father (Luke 5:16).

The wilderness is empty, desert wasteland, a barren place of nothingness, except maybe despair or even terror. Yet the wilderness is where God speaks to us in his mercy – his voice shakes the wilderness itself but speaks tenderly to us, transforming the places where we know trouble into doorways that lead us back to hope again (Psalms 29:8; Hosea 2:14–15).

Our Father marches mercifully through the wilderness towards us (Psalm 68:7). Even in the wastelands and wildernesses, he has got me. He has got you. He is with us. He sees us, he hears us, he speaks tenderly to us. He encircles us, teaches us, keeps us, carries us, covers us and cares for us (Deuteronomy 32:10–12). And he turns the wilderness into pools of water, where we are revived and refreshed, where we can grow into strong trees with deep roots (Psalm 107:35–41; Isaiah 32:15, 41:18–19).

Hope revived

While the wilderness can be a place of failure and falling, it doesn't have to be. It can be the place where we find the Lord and learn that his mercy endures forever (Psalm 136:16, NKJV). It can be where we come to know God at a much deeper level, experiencing his care and provision, and emerging, like Jesus, full of the Holy Spirit and anointed to do the works God has prepared for us. It can be where the pruned become fruitful. God promises us that the wilderness shall bloom, streams will flow in the desert, 'sorrow and sighing shall flee away', and it shall become a 'Way of Holiness', where even fools no longer go astray (Isaiah 35:1–10).

The wilderness can be the very place where God displays his completely undeserved mercy by drawing back his wandering people to himself. That's what we see in Hosea, where the language used about God's wayward people is blunt, with the Lord telling the prophet to 'take to yourself a wife of whoredom and have children of whoredom, for the land commits great whoredom by forsaking the LORD' (Hosea 1:2). This language may be offensive to us in our modern context, but Hosea is to be a living example of the relationship between God and his continually unfaithful, rebellious people.

Hosea is even told to call his daughter 'No Mercy' (Hosea 1:6) as God threatens, briefly, to stop showing mercy to his people. Yet it is in this context that God says he will 'allure her, and bring her into the wilderness'. Why? So he can 'speak tenderly to her' and revive hope (Hosea 2:14–15). We see this in the writings of another prophet, Isaiah. For a 'mere moment', God forsakes his people owing to his 'little wrath' – 'little' compared with his 'great mercies' and 'everlasting kindness' (Isaiah 54:7–8, NKJV). As Matthew Henry summarises it: 'As God is slow to anger, so he is swift to show mercy... The wrath is little, the mercies great; the wrath for a moment, the kindness everlasting.'[1]

Back to Hosea and his unfaithful wife, and we see God's response to our own sinful waywardness. John Piper explains:

He promises to take us into the wilderness. He wants to be alone with us. Why? So that he can speak tenderly to us. Literally, the Hebrew says, so that he can speak 'to her heart'. And when he speaks, he will allure you. He will entice you and woo you... Go with him into the wilderness and listen with your heart. Do not think you are too ugly or too rotten. He knows that his wife is a harlot. That's the meaning of mercy: God is wooing a wife of harlotry.[2]

Imagine how this might play out in a Hollywood movie. It is like the hero of the film – a beautiful, kind, honourable, compassionate man – chasing after a woman who has repeatedly acted with disdain towards him, doing everything she can to wound his heart, with nothing about her that would attract *anyone*, let alone one as outstanding in every way as he is. If we saw this in a film, it wouldn't make sense to us. We would be sitting tensely in our cinema seats, silently urging the guy to walk away, wondering why on earth he would continue to pursue such an unkind, ugly-hearted woman who doesn't even want him.

It is the astonishing, unfathomable mercy of God that he takes us into the wilderness; not to abandon us there, but to win our hearts to him in that place.

He does not desert us in the desert.

He woos us with his tender mercies. He leads us into the wilderness by them, and they follow us all the days of our lives, wherever we go (Exodus 15:13; Psalm 23:6). He races to us with his tender mercies, which bring us comfort and life, even in the wastelands (Psalms 79:8; 119:76–77).

God is very present in the wilderness seasons of our lives, so when we find ourselves in that place, let's not ask, as the Israelites did, 'Can God spread a table in the wilderness?' (Psalm 78:19). Let's trust his character and trust that, even in the desert places, he has prepared a table full of tender mercies for us. And not just for us, but for others too. Because although the mercy of God towards us is not based on our character, but on his, it demands a response from us that will change not just how we think about God, but how we think about ourselves and others.

We are invited to delight in God's mercy, but we mustn't stop there. We are not simply to enjoy his mercy, but to be transformed by it. God calls his people to 'put on tender mercies' (Colossians 3:12, NKJV). We are to cultivate tenderheartedness and a love for mercy that compels us to think differently and act accordingly (1 Peter 3:8).

Part 3
MERCIFUL THINKING

Mercy is at the very heart of God's character. He wants it to be at the heart of ours, too. Our objections to the mercy of God come from the fact that we need to grasp it more thoroughly: to marinate in it and let it mature us into those who really, deeply love mercy.

Loving mercy is an attitude of the heart. A deep understanding of the wonderful, abundant mercy God has shown to us should lead to a joyful anticipation of ways in which we can show mercy to others. Sadly, too often it doesn't. It is so easy to celebrate God's mercy in our own lives while failing to make the connection between receiving his mercy and becoming mercy-bringers to others.

We need to change our thinking. As we have already read in Micah 6:8, God requires us to move beyond gratitude for his mercy and to become people who love showing mercy to others. But it takes hard work.

Despite immersing myself in the mercy of God for several years, my heart and mind are slow to align with God's. My thoughts are becoming more merciful, but they are taking their time.

At the mercy of others

It is often in my knee-jerk reactions that my unmerciful thinking is exposed. While writing this book I received a message on social media from a guy I do not know, asking me why I am not married and do not have children, and informing me that I cannot be fully surrendered to Christ in view of this.

I was livid. *Who does he think he is?* my mind raged, as I started composing various replies in my head. I took screenshots of his message and rushed to send them to a couple of friends, wanting them to jump in on my anger with me.

One of them replied straight away with: 'Lord, have mercy.'
Gah!

I immediately realised my initial reaction had been anything but merciful!

Does the guy deserve my mercy? Not as far as I can see. But that's not the point. If I want to become a follower of Jesus who loves mercy, I need to cultivate a merciful heart that leads to merciful thoughts. I need to concern myself primarily with *my* attitude, not with *his*.

Otherwise, what am I at the mercy of? A stranger's message? In our world of hyperconnectedness, I'm going to be in trouble if I let people I have never met dictate my words and actions.

Our emotions and responses can so easily be at the mercy of other people. As Henri Nouwen wrote: 'A little criticism makes me angry, and a little rejection makes me depressed. A little praise raises my spirits, and a little success excites me. It takes very little to raise me up or thrust me down. Often I am like a small boat on the ocean, completely at the mercy of its waves.'[1]

But when I begin to love mercy the way that God loves mercy, and to train myself so that merciful thinking becomes my default setting, I start to find I am no longer at the mercy of other people. My reactions cease to be shaped by the words or deeds of others, and are shaped instead by the words and deeds of my Father God.

Of course, I do not get this right all the time. I am a work in progress. Thankfully, because he is mercifully patient with us, what God desires from me is progress, not perfection. He is making me more like Jesus one degree at a time (2 Corinthians 3:18). But if I do not apply myself, my progress will grind to a halt. Without pursuing a love of mercy, I am likely to become less merciful, not more.

We do not tend to drift in the direction of mercy. Our hearts do not become more merciful by osmosis. Reading a book on it is not enough. *Writing* a book on it is not enough. We need to soberly assess our thoughts and responses, be honest and humble when we get it wrong, repent of our lack of mercy, and commit ourselves to becoming those who, 'in view of God's mercy', are 'transformed by the renewing of [our] mind[s]' to love and delight in mercy, just as he does (Romans 12:1-3, NIV).

Before we can live merciful lives, we need merciful thinking. And merciful thinking only develops from the overflow of a merciful heart (Luke 6:45; Matthew 12:33–35; Proverbs 4:23). Cultivating merciful thinking involves dismantling some of the lies we have taken on board from the culture around us.

Loving mercy requires recalibrating our hearts. We have deep work to do.

14

Deserving and undeserving

A true love of mercy can only grow when we start to recognise our unmerciful thinking and remove the lies we have allowed to seep into our hearts from the world around us. One of the biggest obstacles to cultivating a merciful heart is the belief that some people are worthy of mercy and some are not. This is the first lie we need to dismantle.

Human nature tends to place people in categories based on what they have done or failed to do. I have allowed media and popular culture narratives to shape my thinking, so that it generally defaults to something along these lines: if you have worked really hard, tried your best and taken every opportunity, you deserve to catch a break and you deserve help from any of us who has the power to help you. If the opposite is true, well, you made your bed...

Jonah had a very clear idea about who deserved God's mercy and who did not. So did the Pharisees. Our own concept of the deserving and undeserving may not be as brazen as theirs but, if we are truly honest with ourselves, I believe we would all confess that there are some people we think we should show mercy to and others we think we should not.

It might be a particular group of people – those who are not grateful for the kindness and compassion they receive, those who demand support as if it is their right, those who should have known better for one reason or another, or those who have repeatedly made the same mistakes.

Biblically speaking, are we supposed to show mercy to *everyone*? Surely that can't be right?

David and Mephibosheth

There are two stories in the Bible that have particularly helped me to explore this. First, we have the account of David and Mephibosheth in 2 Samuel 9:3–11):

> And the king said, 'Is there not still someone of the house of Saul, that I may show the kindness of God to him?' Ziba said to the king, 'There is still a son of Jonathan; he is crippled in his feet.' ...Then King David sent and brought him... And Mephibosheth the son of Jonathan, son of Saul, came to David and fell on his face and paid homage. And David said, 'Mephibosheth!' And he answered, 'Behold, I am your servant.' And David said to him, 'Do not fear, for I will show you kindness for the sake of your father Jonathan, and I will restore to you all the land of Saul your father, and you shall eat at my table always.' And he paid homage and said, 'What is your servant, that you should show regard for a dead dog such as I?'
>
> Then the king called Ziba, Saul's servant, and said to him, 'All that belonged to Saul and to all his house I have given to your master's grandson. And you and your sons and your servants shall till the land for him and shall bring in the produce, that your master's grandson may have bread to eat. But Mephibosheth your master's grandson shall always eat at my table.' ...So Mephibosheth ate at David's table, like one of the king's sons...

When I think about Mephibosheth, I feel compassion. It comes naturally to me to want to show mercy to someone like him. We learn from an earlier part of the story that Mephibosheth became 'lame in both his feet' when he was just five years old. Perceiving his life to be in danger, his nurse picked him up to flee to safety with him, and as she hurried to get away, Mephibosheth fell and injured his feet, becoming disabled (2 Samuel 4:4).

In the society and culture in which he lived, being unable to walk meant he could not provide for himself and his family. He would have been reliant on other people because of what had happened to him when he was a child.

I find it pretty easy to extend mercy to Mephibosheth, because he was in an accident at such a young age. It wasn't his fault; he was a victim of circumstances. On top of that, I like the fact he is humble and grateful for David's kindness to him, bowing down and saying: 'What is your servant, that you should look upon such a dead dog as I?'

He doesn't expect David's compassion or demand his kindness. He knows he has no claim to it, so he is appropriately grateful. I like the way he recognises that he does not deserve David's mercy.

I do not feel moved to show mercy to people who are entitled and do not express sufficient gratitude. But this combination in a person – being a blameless victim and expressing humility – quickly stirs my heart to mercy.

The partying prodigal

But not everyone is like Mephibosheth. Many of us have stories that are more complicated than his. That is where our second example, which we find in Luke 15:11–24 (NIV), comes in:

Jesus continued: 'There was a man who had two sons. The younger one said to his father, "Father, give me my share of the estate." So he divided his property between them.

'Not long after that, the younger son got together all he had, set off for a distant country and there squandered his wealth in wild living. After he had spent everything, there was a severe famine in that whole country, and he began to be in need. So he went and hired himself out to a citizen of that country, who sent him to his fields to feed pigs. He longed to fill his stomach with the pods that the pigs were eating, but no one gave him anything.

'When he came to his senses, he said, "How many of my father's hired servants have food to spare, and here I am starving to death! I will set out and go back to my father and say to him: Father, I have sinned against heaven and against you. I am no longer worthy to be called your son; make me like one of your hired servants." So he got up and went to his father.

'But while he was still a long way off, his father saw him and was filled with compassion for him; he ran to his son, threw his arms round him and kissed him.

'The son said to him, "Father, I have sinned against heaven and against you. I am no longer worthy to be called your son."

'But the father said to his servants, "Quick! Bring the best robe and put it on him. Put a ring on his finger and sandals on his feet. Bring the fattened calf and kill it. Let's have a feast and celebrate. For this son of mine was dead and is alive again; he was lost and is found." So they began to celebrate.

The prodigal son stands in stark contrast to Mephibosheth. He, too, is facing dire circumstances – he is starving to death during a famine – but his situation is entirely of his own making. He isn't a victim of circumstances beyond his control. His arrogance and sense of entitlement brought him here. He insulted his dad by asking for money so he could get away from his family. And then he squandered it on parties and prostitutes (Luke 15:13, 30).

If I start to imagine these two men turning up at my church in need of a food parcel, my heart responds very differently to their stories. The prodigal caused his own poverty. Therefore, if I am honest about my thinking, he does not deserve my help. And if I decide to help him anyway, how do I know he won't just squander it?

So now I have a problem.

When I find myself quickly and definitively categorising people into two camps – those who deserve mercy and those who do not – it reveals that my heart is just like Jonah's after all: quick to forget that I did not deserve the incredible mercy I have been shown.

Selective mercy

It turns out that Jonah and I are not the only ones who are selective with our mercy. The prodigal son's older brother is just like us (Luke 15:28–30). He is angry at his dad's mercy, just as Jonah was angry with God. He refuses to go to the party to celebrate, just as Jonah left Nineveh to sulk (Jonah 4:5).

Similarly, the Pharisees seem unable to cope with the mercy of God when it is extended to those they deem undeserving. In fact, Jesus tells the parable about the prodigal son in response to the Pharisees' grumbling as 'a lot of men and women of questionable reputation' drew close to Jesus (Luke 15:1–2, MSG). They couldn't understand why Jesus would eat with tax collectors and sinners, and when he healed on the Sabbath they were furious (Matthew 9:11; Luke 6:11).

While the Pharisees topped the Premier League when it came to being anti-mercy, even those closest to Jesus were not immune. Two of his twelve disciples – brothers James and John – were given the nickname 'Sons of Thunder' by Jesus (Mark 3:17), possibly because their response to people who didn't receive Jesus was: 'Lord, do you want us to tell fire to come down from heaven and consume them?' (Luke 9:54) – as if they had ever seen Jesus do anything like that!

There is no shortage of people in the Bible who had known the mercy of God for themselves, or should have been well acquainted with it, but who did not love the mercy of God when they saw it extended to others.

We are just like the world around us when we think that people need to show us why they deserve our mercy before we can decide whether or not they are worthy of it. It is worldly thinking that looks at someone's behaviour and responds to that. Christians are called to be different. Our mercy is not supposed to be based on the person in front of us, but on Jesus and the example he has set for us.

God is not like us. His mercy is not given only after we have qualified for it. That is not the way things work in his kingdom. We get the order wrong. Behave well enough and you can have mercy – that is the way of the world. Receive mercy, which will empower you to thrive – that is the way of the kingdom. We need to turn our thinking upside-down. God's thoughts are not our thoughts, but he wants our thoughts to be increasingly shaped by his. That will change our view not just on who deserves mercy and who does not, but on the whole concept of deserving and undeserving.

15

Father-like thinking

When we read about Mephibosheth and the prodigal son, we tend to cast ourselves in their roles. I am Mephibosheth, the one who was powerless to help myself but is now welcome to eat at the king's table for all my days. I am the prodigal, who wandered far from God, indulging in whatever I thought would bring me fulfilment and satisfaction, but have now been embraced and drawn into my heavenly Father's family.

These are helpful ways to read these stories. It is true: you and I were Mephibosheth, and we were the prodigal son. But once we gave our lives to Jesus and became his disciples, our role in these stories changed. We are no longer Mephibosheth; we are no longer the prodigal son. We now have the extraordinary privilege of becoming like the father figures in these stories and, even more incredibly, of becoming like our Father in heaven.

When it comes to mercy, the focal point of our thinking needs to change. We no longer look at the person in front of us; nor do we look around at what society would say about them. Now we look up, at who God is and how he treats us. That, and only that, is the basis for our mercy, our compassion, our gentleness, our soft-heartedness towards each person he brings across our path. Our practical support may look different from person to person, but the heart motivation should be the same each time.

We show mercy because he has shown us mercy.

Maturing as a Christian means imitating Jesus, being conformed to his image, and becoming more and more like our Father, because Jesus and the Father are one. This is the high calling God had in mind when he predestined us to be his. Jesus has called us to: 'Be merciful, even as your Father is merciful' (Luke 6:36). We are called to live out our new identity as the merciful children of the Father of mercies (2 Corinthians 1:3).

Proactive mercy

There is still more to learn from Mephibosheth and the prodigal son to help us with this because, while they stand in stark contrast to one another, the father figures in each story act in exactly the same way: with mercy. Just like our Father.

First, notice that both King David and the prodigal's father are *actively* looking to show mercy. David does not wait to see if an opportunity lands in his lap. He makes it happen by asking if there is anyone left of Saul's house to whom he can show kindness, or more specifically *God's* kindness and mercy.[1] He intentionally seeks to reflect the Father's heart to someone.

Similarly, we can assume that the father of the prodigal son is actively on the lookout for his son, because he sees him coming home when he is still a long way off. (Note that the father shows the same mercy to the older brother. Later in the parable, he goes looking for him and pleads with him to come to the party.)

Both father figures take the initiative. Neither seems preoccupied with thoughts of whether the recipient is deserving or undeserving. The starting place is a heart that desires to show mercy.

Mephibosheth would have undoubtedly approached King David with fear. The custom at this time was to execute swiftly any last surviving heir of the previous dynasty, since they could make a claim to the throne. That is why Mephibosheth's nurse tried to flee with him in the first place. As the grandson of Saul and the son of Jonathan, both of whom had died in battle, Mephibosheth had a rightful claim to become king of Israel if no one else from the family survived. David did not have to show him mercy. In fact, David should have killed him.

And in the case of the prodigal son, what would it have been like for him as he trekked home, wondering whether his father would allow him back as a servant or turn him away completely?

When I know that I have sinned against God, I have to work hard to remind myself that I can still boldly approach him, because what comes naturally to me is to assume that I will be shunned or punished, at least for a time. I wonder how nervous the prodigal felt, running over in his mind what he would say to his dad, agonising over what response he might receive, adrenalin ramping up as he got closer and closer to home. What must it have been like as he saw his father running towards him? As we saw in Part 1, the father doesn't even let the son get through the speech he has rehearsed – he is too busy embracing him.

Incredible mercy!

Above and beyond

But the father figures in these two stories go further still. Their mercy isn't just demonstrated in welcoming and accepting Mephibosheth and the prodigal, though that in itself would have been wonderfully gracious. They go above and beyond by being lavish with their mercy. They really do seem to revel and delight in it.

Instead of treating Mephibosheth as a threat to his kingdom, David restores all of Saul's land to him, and commands Ziba, his sons and his servants to tend it, so that Mephibosheth will have food (2 Samuel 9:7–10). Considering that Saul had tried to kill David (more than once!), this is already exceptionally merciful on David's part.

But then he takes it to another level when he invites Mephibosheth to eat at his table every day for the rest of his life. This is an extraordinary act of mercy. David has already ensured that Mephibosheth will be well cared for and supplied with all he needs. In that sense, it's an unnecessary kindness for David to draw

Mephibosheth into the royal family. Yet here he is, treating as a son someone who could have been seen as an enemy. What a beautiful picture of our heavenly Father's mercy towards us.

This is exactly how God wants his people to live – with a countercultural mercy that loves our enemies, does good even to those who could harm us, and draws in those whom others would tell us to despise (Luke 6:27–36; Matthew 5:38–48). David could have put forward several good reasons why he should kill Mephibosheth. Likewise, we may have strong grounds for refusing to be merciful to some of the people we come across, but our solid reasons (even when added together) do not stack up against the one overriding reason we have to show mercy, which is that we ourselves have been shown outrageous mercy that we did not deserve.

When we refuse to show mercy, we reflect the world around us, not the God who has rescued us. Jesus made this point plainly when he said in Luke 6:32–36 (NIV):

> "If you love those who love you, what credit is that to you? Even sinners love those who love them. And if you do good to those who are good to you, what credit is that to you? Even sinners do that... But love your enemies, do good to them, and lend to them without expecting to get anything back. Then your reward will be great, and you will be children of the Most High, because he is kind to the ungrateful and wicked. Be merciful, just as your Father is merciful."

This is one of the markers that sets Jesus-followers apart from the world around us: we show mercy to those whom most people would write off as undeserving. It may look foolish to our society. People may say we are being exploited, that the recipients of our mercy are taking advantage of us. Sometimes that will be true – possibly more often than not. But our mercy is not built on whether it makes sense in our culture. Its foundation is the incredible mercy of the Father.

The prodigal son's dad could have welcomed him back as a servant, and that would have been gracious enough by most people's reckoning. He could have given him the essentials – clean clothes, food, shelter – and that would have been kind, considering his son had effectively said: 'I wish you were dead' by asking for his inheritance, and then gone off and 'devoured [his] property with prostitutes', squandering half of his father's wealth (Luke 15:30).

But instead, the father does something astonishing – he throws a party for his party-loving son. This prodigal who ran off to enjoy wild living now receives an extravagant celebration in his honour. The wayward one who asked for his father's riches and threw them all away is now dressed from head to toe in clothes befitting a precious son. He is wrapped in the best robe and given the family ring. The fattened calf is prepared for him to eat. The father gives the prodigal the very things he had requested and wasted – the son receives more than he had before.

What a wonderful father to show such abundant, undeserved mercy!

Blame and shame

In the context of an unforgiving cancel culture, this is hard to compute. We are used to polarising headlines that tell us why those around us don't deserve mercy, compassion or even help. Greg Haslam writes in *The Jonah Complex* about what happened when notorious serial killer Jeffrey Dahmer became a Christian and was baptised: 'The surprising news of his conversion became widely known and vilified as a cheap shot to elicit public sympathy. The media went into a frenzy of protest and angry reports… One striking headline in the press asked in bold type, WHO IS RESPONSIBLE FOR THIS OUTRAGE? And, of course, the shocking and unexpected final answer to that question is, "God"!'[2]

There is no one alive right now who is beyond God's mercy. But there are many people who are beyond ours. Can you imagine the headlines that would be written about the prodigal's dad today? 'Doting dad duped by deadbeat son' perhaps? The tabloids, in particular, might scream in block capitals: 'WHO DOES RECKLESS SON THINK HE IS?' while the subheading might read: 'Prodigal swans home to exploit his old man.'

One area of British life in which our cynicism about people is particularly pronounced is the welfare system. While it may have recently gone out of fashion for national newspapers to run headlines lamenting 'skivers', 'scroungers', 'dossers', 'shirkers' and 'fiddlers', judging those on benefits as 'workshy' and pitting us (hardworking, 'decent' citizens) against them,[3] these narratives have become deeply embedded in people's minds and pervasive in British society today. Much of the Western world has imbibed similar outlooks, even though they are based mostly on false narratives and the myth that if we just work hard enough, we can achieve whatever we aspire to. We believe that if you haven't 'made it' – if you haven't reached your goals or, worse still, you are stuck in poverty – it must be because you didn't try hard enough.

Sometimes that's true, but the idea that we all create our own success or failure is built on the assumption that we all start in the same place, which is clearly false. Some are born into privilege; others have the odds stacked against them from the start. Neither does it take into account the complexity of most people's lives. When I was trapped in overwhelming debt, for example, it was for a number of reasons. Some factors were beyond my control, *and* I made some bad decisions. Isn't that true of most of us? Few of us are *entirely* victims of circumstance. Few of us are *entirely* at fault when our lives are hard. Usually, it's a mix of both: 'x' happened to me, then I foolishly did 'y', and now I'm stuck at 'z'.

But the glorious reality of God's mercy is that it isn't based on a mathematical calculation about how much we got ourselves into a mess versus what percentage was beyond our control.

No record of wrongs

Jonah, the Pharisees, the disciples, the prodigal's older brother, the world around us, and even our own hearts may question whether we deserve God's mercy. Others may join with the devil in accusing us of causing our own misery.

But thankfully, wonderfully, God never says that to us.

When we call out to him, he doesn't tot up all the things we couldn't help in one column and all the foolish mistakes we made in another. God's response to Mephibosheths and prodigals is the same, because it's not based on who they are, what they have done or what they have failed to do. It is based on the fact that he is and always will be the Father of mercies.

One of the most extraordinary twists in the gospel story is that we are invited to become just like him. As we start out on this journey towards transformed hearts, it will make us uncomfortable. It is hard to swim against the social tide that tells us to be cautious about the people in whom we choose to invest our time, money, energy and support. As we seek to love mercy, we may find that attitudes we have held for years start to bother us, requiring us to repent of our lack of mercy, our lack of Christlikeness. We may not change the minds of others, even other Christians. Changing our own minds is hard enough.

Are we willing to have our thinking so thoroughly transformed that we shed the unmerciful thoughts we have about others and start to think like the Father of mercies? This is the exciting adventure the Holy Spirit wants to lead us into.

16

Planks and specks

If 'mercy triumphs over judgement' (James 2:13), it makes sense that one of the enemies of merciful thinking is judgemental thinking. How easy it is for our thoughts to be filled with the latter!

I mentioned in the Introduction that if your church ran a course on how to be judgemental, I would not need to attend. It seems to be hardwired into my thought patterns. Just as we need to learn that our role has changed from being Mephibosheths and prodigals to becoming like the Father, many of us also need to learn that we are not called to be judgemental but to be merciful.

Billy Graham said: 'It is the Holy Spirit's job to convict, God's job to judge and my job to love.'[1]

I often get confused about my role. If I'm honest, I quite enjoy trying to bring a bit of conviction to those around me, especially when I'm reading a verse in the Bible or listening to a point in a sermon that I think they really need to respond to!

I'm sure I am not alone in this. If it were not a common experience, Jesus could have skipped the part in the Sermon on the Mount where he said: 'Do not judge, or you too will be judged... Why do you look at the speck of sawdust in your brother's eye and pay no attention to the plank in your own eye?' (Matthew 7:1–3, NIV).

Other people's lives

Media scrutiny is a vital part of any healthy democracy. I trained and worked as a journalist, so I place a high value on freedom of the press and the importance of impartial news agencies holding the powerful to account. But we live in an extremely judgemental society where much of our public discourse is gossip dressed up as news, which invites us to form opinions on people and situations we barely know anything about. We can even believe the lie that somehow we have a right to pass judgement on others.

When Martin Charlesworth and I were writing our first book, *The Myth of the Undeserving Poor*, we wanted to find out what shaped the attitudes of UK Christians towards those in poverty in our local settings. We found that whichever media outlet we turn to weekly or more regularly has a greater impact on our opinions about poverty in our neighbourhoods and nation than God's word. Our thoughts are more likely to be shaped by news headlines than Bible verses.[2]

The Scriptures are clear that what we meditate on matters. That is why we are instructed to take our thoughts captive (2 Corinthians 10:5). If we think we are immune to the narratives that shape the world around us, we are – to be blunt – foolish. Over the last year, I have rationed my social media consumption to half an hour a week, partly because I was losing count of the number of hours I had wasted tunnelling down a rabbit hole of posts and articles about people I had never met.

We live in a culture that very much concerns itself with other people's lives. We lurch from one scandal to another, poring over details not just about who is alleged to have done what, but also of what other people we do not know think about it. And this lures us into joining in with the polarisation that is such a defining feature of our society, where we pick sides and pronounce judgements without any sure and certain facts.

I have been tested in this recently by being asked to give my instant, honest responses to the names of people in the public eye. It went like this:

On hearing the name of one member of the British royal family, I said: 'Protected by privilege – no smoke without fire.' When another was mentioned, my response was a much more sympathetic: 'Poor guy, he's just worried for his family.'

When a famous pastor was named, I accused him of arrogance and questioned whether he should still be allowed to lead a church. When a second pastor was brought up, I expressed far more concern about his personal wellbeing, even though it is highly likely that he has caused just as much damage to people as the first.

Two recently disgraced TV presenters were named – I responded with condemnation for one and compassion for the other.

I don't know any of these people. None has been convicted of a crime, but I harbour instinctive judgements about each one, based on a combination of what I have read online and my own issues, triggers and experiences, which cause me to have a bias in certain situations.

When it comes to people in the public eye, it is helpful to remember that many of them are completely at the mercy of public opinion. Their whole lives can either rise or fall based on what is written about them, with careers and relationships left in tatters and a ripple effect that we barely care about as our heads are quickly turned by the next scandal.

Like the culture around me, my heart is prone to judgement. So, as a follower of Christ, I must check my attitude and choose to lean in to mercy. In the absence of evidence, merciful thinking assumes the best, not the worst. And when the facts are known, merciful thinking is able to hope for justice for those who have *been wronged* and redemption for those who have *done wrong*.

In a world where we tend to polarise our mercy towards just one party – usually the one most like us – it is countercultural to show and hope for mercy towards both parties.

Mind your business

Merciful thinking can mean choosing *not* to think about something. It might involve avoiding reams of social media posts about a person or situation. The apostle Paul wrote: 'You should mind your own business' (1 Thessalonians 4:11, NIV). This may seem like such a small step of obedience, but it can be a very difficult one in a culture where so many people's lives are paraded before us as if they *are* our business.

We need to apply it within church settings, too. How often has a brother or sister in Christ shared something about someone else 'so you can pray'? I have a friend who, at the slightest hint of gossip, jumps in with, 'Don't tell me! I don't need to know.' It's annoying sometimes, because it makes me feel guilty even if I'm not about to say something I shouldn't! But I have learned from her to do likewise. It is better to pre-emptively cut off a conversation than to get a little taste of a juicy gossip morsel that whets my appetite for more (Proverbs 18:8, 26:22).

I am actively trying to curb my curiosity about situations that do not concern me. I pray about it often and frequently remind myself that I do not need to know about this or that – things that are to do with other people, and not my business. As I actively steer my heart towards mercy over judgement, I find that I am regularly drawn to the final chapter of John's Gospel, where Peter wants to know what will happen to John. Just as Jesus replied to Peter, I hear the Holy Spirit tenderly whispering to me: 'What is that to you?' (John 21:22).

Just to be clear: Christians *are* meant to be in a church community where we speak into each other's lives. Each of us should be discipling those who are less mature in their faith, and being discipled by those who are more mature. Every time I hang out with one particular friend, she asks me how my heart is doing. I answer honestly. We confess sinful attitudes and behaviours to each other, and we definitely see it as our responsibility to help each other grow in loving and obeying Jesus. Another friend is currently holding me accountable for close to a dozen habits and thought patterns I am keen to keep or kick.

We need other believers to speak into our lives. Among God's greatest gifts of mercy are the friends who walk alongside us in the various seasons of our lives. We are to embrace those relationships with godly saints who have the courage to correct us when we need it. As David writes in Psalm 141:5 (NABRE): 'Let a righteous person strike me; it is mercy if he reproves me.'

Though I might pretend otherwise, I can tell the difference between godly discipleship and concerning myself with matters that are not my business. If we are honest, we know when we are gossiping and being judgemental. When I go ahead anyway, it is usually because I choose to, not because I don't realise what I'm doing.

We must not minimise the importance of this. In Isaiah 58 – where the Lord is calling his people back to true fasting – we find, nestled in the middle of verses about feeding the hungry and providing shelter for the homeless, God's command to remove from our midst 'the pointing of the finger, and speaking wickedness' (Isaiah 58:9).

When we are judgemental and finger-pointing, we resemble our accuser more than our Redeemer. Jesus was stern about this with the Pharisees and scribes, telling them that they were not children of the Father, but of the devil (John 8:44).

Mercy triumphs over judgement in our hearts and in our thinking when we remember that: 'There is none who does good, not even one' (Psalm 14:3). As Bonhoeffer wrote from prison: 'Nothing that we despise in the other man is entirely absent from ourselves.'[3]

Merciful thinking changes the direction of our questions away from judgements about the sins and motives of others to asking what is at work in our own hearts: 'Search *me*, O God, and know *my* heart! Try *me* and know *my* thoughts! And see if there be any grievous way in *me*, and lead *me* in the way everlasting!' (Psalm 139:23–24, emphasis mine).

We are on the journey to thinking mercifully when we start to deliberately shuffle away from conversations where we might be tempted to lap up words that tear others down, indulge in speculation and celebrate another's downfall.

It takes effort and energy to train ourselves to think mercifully. But when we invite the Spirit to develop in us the mind of Christ (1 Corinthians 2:16), we find that we stop loving judgement and start loving mercy. When the children of God seek to imitate the Father of mercies, mercy begins to triumph over judgement.

17

Mercy's version of events

Rejected, hurting, insecure, disappointed, incapable of consistently obeying Jesus. Those were once the keywords in my version of my story. If I tell my own story with more judgement than mercy, is it any wonder that I do the same to others?

God is the only person who knows the full extent of my sin. He knows every noble thought and every evil one. He knows when my intentions are good and when they are selfish. He knows me at my best and at my worst. He sees my life from every vantage point. He understands what brings my heart joy and what makes me lash out in anger, and why. He is the only One who knows my heart, and yours.

And he is so beautifully merciful in how he tells our stories.

My messy past

I only started to grasp this a couple of years ago. One day, during a particularly difficult season in my life, I was reflecting on my journey of faith. Looking back over more than a quarter of a century of knowing and wrestling with Jesus, I saw a lot of pain and bad decisions. I was lamenting to God: 'When I look back over my life, Father, all I see is mess after mess after mess.'

I was referring to my own mistakes: times I had wandered away from God; decisions I regretted; words I wished I could take back; actions I longed to undo; even whole periods of time I wished I could erase. I was also thinking about times when I got caught up in other people's mess and became collateral damage in someone else's story.

As I sorrowed over the pitted landscape of my Christian life, I heard the tender yet firm words of the Father, whispering into the depths of my heart: 'When I look back over your life, I don't see mess after mess after mess. I see mercy after mercy after mercy.'

It made me cry with joy, as it opened the eyes of my heart to see, to a greater depth, just how astonishingly merciful God is.

The Father of mercies does not look at our lives in snapshots, as we tend to. He sees the whole. He sees the end from the beginning, he sees our hearts, he discerns our thoughts from afar, he knows our words before we speak them out, he is acquainted with all our ways (Psalm 139). He understands us more intimately and intricately than we know ourselves.

We need to dismantle the lie that our lives are summed up by a moment, a mistake or a season. As Christians, we must hold on to and hold out the truth that, while there is breath in our lungs, there is hope. Until we die, redemption is always possible, always available and always God's desired outcome. Failure does not have to have the final word.

Merciful summaries

As we cultivate a love for mercy in our hearts and minds, we have the privilege of telling other people's stories with a kindness and a gentleness like God's. But it requires renewed thinking.

When I think about David, his compassion towards Mephibosheth isn't the first story that comes to mind. Occasionally it is his encounter with Goliath, but most often it is his adultery with Bathsheba and the subsequent murder of her husband, Uriah. If you asked me to sum up David's story, I would probably start with: 'He was an adulterer and a murderer.' And yet, twice in the Holy Spirit-inspired word of God, David is described as a man after God's own heart (1 Samuel 13:14; Acts 13:22). The first time is before David committed these sins, but the second is afterwards. The Bible even describes David – after telling us of his sins – as a man whose heart was 'wholly true to the LORD his God' (1 Kings 11:4), which does not make sense to me at all!

But God sees the heart, he sees the whole story, and he gives us his merciful summary of David's life.

David isn't the only example. When I read about his son Solomon, I think of him as really foolish. He was granted wisdom and wealth by God, yet he chased after hundreds of women and let them draw his heart away from the Lord his God, even towards other gods. The Bible tells us that although Solomon became a king like no other, and was dearly loved by God (Nehemiah 13:26), he did what was evil in the sight of the Lord (1 Kings 11:6). Yet, more than 3,000 years after Solomon was born, he is still revered as the wisest person who ever lived. Even Jesus holds Solomon up as an example of wisdom when chastising the Pharisees (Matthew 12:42). Solomon started out so well, but he did not end well. Yet, in God's mercy, we know him as the epitome of wisdom.

Hebrews 11 features many such strange versions of events. Take Sarah, for example, who is commended for her faith in God, which led her to conceive in her old age 'because she believed the One who made a promise would do what he said' (Hebrews 11:11, MSG). This makes me want to say to the writer of the letter to the Hebrews, in bewilderment: 'Excuse me, she *what*?' When I flick back in my Bible, just to check I'm remembering correctly, what I find there is not a story of Sarah's incredible faith in God, but that first she laughed at his promise, and then she lied about laughing (Genesis 18:12–15).

Other people listed in Hebrews 11 as examples of great faith include Gideon, Samson and Barak, all of whom I would be tempted to define as weak. Yet God seems to have a different take on their lives. He sums up their stories with words far more merciful than mine would be.

It is the same with Peter in the Gospels. Instead of calling him a denier, a betrayer or a failure – the guy who couldn't even stay awake to pray for Jesus when he was 'sorrowful and troubled... even to death' (Matthew 26:37–43) – Jesus speaks the word 'rock' over him (Matthew 16:18).

Similarly, after Jesus has risen from the dead, he speaks merciful words over the eleven disciples. An angel has just appeared to the two Marys at the tomb, telling them to 'go quickly and tell his *disciples* that he has risen from the dead', but as they run to do so, Jesus himself meets them on the way and says: 'Go and tell my *brothers* to go to Galilee, and there they will see me' (Matthew 28:1–10, ESV, italics mine). Terry Virgo points out that these are 'amazing resurrection words': 'Not "Go tell those failures, deserters, deniers".' Once followers, later even called "friends", but now his "brothers"... What grace!'[1]

A better story

God tells our stories differently from how others might tell them, and differently from how we ourselves might tell them.

Before God spoke into the way I see my own story – transforming it from a tale of mess upon mess to one of mercy upon mercy – there were a number of labels I used to define myself. Over a period of time, I asked Jesus to speak into each one.

Where I used to call myself 'wayward', he called me 'tenacious'.

In place of 'prone to wander', he showed me that I am, by his grace, 'prone to coming back'.

He erased the word 'broken' and replaced it with 'rebuilt, renewed and restored', because that is what Jesus loves to do in the lives of those who have known poverty, heartbreak, captivity and grief (Isaiah 61:1–3). More mercifully still, he took me beyond this, transforming me into someone who rebuilds, renews and restores others (Isaiah 61:4).

Where I saw myself as incapable of being faithful to God, he told me that in Christ I am an 'oak of righteousness' (Isaiah 61:3) who brings him glory!

When one of my friends told me how she keeps slipping into a bad habit she has been trying to break for years, she described herself as a failure. I was shocked, because for a long time I have thought of her as a role model in persistence. I pointed out to her: 'You keep getting back up, dusting yourself off and trying again. You are not a failure. You are an overcomer.'

Labels are powerful. But the Father of mercies is in the habit of erasing labels we have been given by others or have written over ourselves. He rewrites our stories and who we are with his merciful and tender labels. Whatever banner you have lived under – and I have made my home under banners of 'broken', 'rejected', 'abandoned', 'worthless' and many others in my life – *his* banner over you is love (Song of Solomon 2:4).

It doesn't mean the other words had or have no truth to them. David did commit adultery; Peter did deny Jesus. I have been rejected, and I have been prone to wander. Neither does it mean that God is oblivious to our sin, mess, pain and brokenness. He is more aware of those things than we are!

But he writes a better story. The blood of Jesus speaks a better word over us (Hebrews 12:24). It is not just our past that is rewritten in his mercy; he also writes a more glorious future for us. In his incredible kindness, he says: 'You shall no more be termed Forsaken...' [or 'abandoned', 'rejected', 'prone to wander', 'wayward', 'broken', 'worthless', or whatever labels have been placed on you by yourself or other people] 'but you shall be called My Delight Is in Her' (Isaiah 62:4).

His delight is in me!

His delight is in you!

Isn't that astonishing and wonderful? My old labels have gone. My story has been rewritten by God using the indelible ink of his mercy. And in his hands I am not rejected; I am restored, and a restorer. My story has changed and my role in the story has changed. The same is true for you.

Now we get to be mercy-bringers who retell the stories of others, erasing their labels and supporting them to see who they are and *whose* they are. We get to see people with the eyes of mercy, just as our Father sees them.

Speaking mercifully

But we need to train ourselves to do this. From what we post about others on social media to the subtle ways we influence one friend's opinion of another, we must start by acknowledging that we are prone to telling other people's stories in snapshots, and are often more likely to highlight the worst rather than the very best.

This can play out in a number of ways in Christian circles. For example, when we hear someone we know receiving praise that is not merited (in our opinion), we might give a subtle look or express a tight-lipped 'hmmm' that conveys our disagreement. We may not want to actually say anything dismissive – we might look bad if we did that – but we do want the person giving the praise to know that the person they are praising may not be as worthy as they think.

This can be a particular temptation for church leaders and those very committed to the church when members move on to a new fellowship. Do we speak well when people leave? For example: 'He's a great guy, really passionate about Jesus and those in poverty. He found our church a bit too middle-class, so he moved to one on an estate down the road. I think he'll really be able to flourish in all that God has put on his heart there.' Or do we offer a version of events that is perhaps more a reflection of our own insecurities? For example: 'I think she's changed churches a few times. She was quite opinionated from the start. I'm not sure that anything we might do for those in need would be enough for her.'

People are complex. Many of us think in stark contrasts of black and white. Truthfully, I don't know how to reconcile the fact that a vital person in my early spiritual formation is now a convicted paedophile. What would it look like for me to tell his story mercifully? I don't know for certain, but I imagine it would involve speaking highly of his positive impact on my faith *and* calling out his abuse for the evil that it is.

Our culture struggles to hold in tension the fact that good and gifted people are capable of atrocities, while even those who carry out the vilest acts are not beyond the redemption and mercy of God. This is offensive and scandalous to those who do not understand the offensiveness of their own sin and the scandal of God's mercy towards them. Polarisation says you are either on the right side or the wrong side. Cancel culture holds no space for restoration.

But those who know the mercy of God, and are developing merciful hearts like his, know that the fault line between good and evil runs through every human heart.[2] This empowers us to tell our stories, and other people's stories, the way God does – not hiding the worst, not minimising the harm caused, not making excuses, not defending or even presenting mitigating factors, which God never does. But being able to see the worst and still believe there is hope, as God may yet write a better story – one of redemption and mercy.

God is in the habit of retelling and rewriting our stories, and of showing us who we really are. We are not at liberty to write anyone off. Instead, we are to show, in the way we speak and write about others, that we are a people of redemption, a people who once 'had not received mercy, but now... have received mercy' (1 Peter 2:10) and have had our stories wonderfully rewritten by it.

18

Your life is not about you

People who knew me in my twenties sometimes remind me that, back then, I was rarely seen without my baseball cap. Pulled down low so I could avoid making eye contact, my cap was the signature item in a wardrobe of clothing designed to make me feel I could hide. I was plagued by fear and insecurity, and would beat myself up because I couldn't seem to shake them. Despite God graciously drawing me back to him after a few years of running away, I carried a deep sense of shame as I imagined everyone in church knew about the mess I had made. The baseball cap was like a security blanket, enabling me to avoid the gaze of those around me.

My cap symbolised wanting to hide away in the shadows, but the headwear God gives his people is for an entirely different purpose.

The Father has crowned us with tender mercies (Psalm 103:4, NKJV).

When we begin to think mercifully, the way we think about ourselves and our role in the lives of those around us changes dramatically. We are made to be people who display the splendour of the Lord, bringing him glory by pointing others towards his magnificent mercy. We can showcase the beauty of God to those around us because we are now clothed in beauty instead of ashes, joy instead of mourning, garments of praise instead of despair, and crowns set with the sparkling jewels of his tender mercies (Isaiah 61:3).

Merciful thinking takes us beyond dropping our ungodly attitudes about deserving and undeserving, beyond dealing with our own planks first, beyond a new kindness in how we tell the stories of others. It moves us into a humble realisation that God has raised us up and put us on display, so that people will be drawn to him. Our lives are not our own. Contrary to what the world around us tells us, our lives are not about us.

As Christians, we are not the central characters in our stories. We are adorned with beautiful crowns that should be visible to those around us; not so they gaze at us, but so they wonder and marvel at the Father of the tender mercies we display.

Dazzling crowns

Today is Saturday 6 May 2023, and as I write the coronation of King Charles III is taking place at Westminster Abbey in London. As part of that historic occasion, the St Edward's Crown will be placed on the king's head. The 360-year-old crown is made from solid 22-carat gold. It is more than 30cm (1ft) tall and weighs more than 2kg (5lbs), which might be one of the reasons it is worn for less than an hour before it is returned to its home at the Tower of London![1] It is set with 444 jewels and gemstones, and every element of the crown is symbolic – from the gold beads that lead up to the cross that sits at the top, to the trim at the base.

Coronations are not the only occasions that involve a crown. When Queen Elizabeth II was lying in state, a different crown – the Imperial State – rested on top of her coffin. Although the Imperial State Crown is supposedly less precious and impressive than the St Edward's Crown, it features almost 3,000 diamonds, as well as pearls, sapphires, emeralds and rubies.[2] It is perhaps the most visually dazzling of all the crowns associated with the British monarchy. Yet it is also the most common, if a crown can be called common, because it is worn regularly at the state opening of Parliament and on other formal occasions.

Crowns symbolise status, honour, power and authority.[3] They are grand and ornate, reflecting the dignity and rule of the person who wears them. They attract attention – they are made to be noticed;

to draw the eye in wonder and reverence; to let everyone know they are in the presence of royalty.

Several crowns are mentioned in the Bible, but they are very different from the crowns on display at the Tower of London. Jesus was made to wear a crown of thorns (Matthew 27:29; Mark 15:17; John 19:2–5) – in mockingly stark contrast to the crowns of kings and queens. Around 700 years beforehand, God had promised his people through the prophet Isaiah that one day, after the Messiah had come, the Lord himself would be 'a crown of glory, and a diadem of beauty, to the remnant of his people' and that we would also be 'a crown of beauty in the hand of the LORD, and a royal diadem in the hand of [our] God' (Isaiah 28:5, 62:3).

This is reflected in the New Testament, where we are told to train as those competing for 'an imperishable *crown*'; those who are waiting to be awarded 'the crown of righteousness', 'the crown of life' and 'the unfading crown of glory' (1 Corinthians 9:25, NKJV; 2 Timothy 4:8; James 1:12 and Revelation 2:10; 1 Peter 5:4). This is the crown we will have when we see Jesus face to face, when we worship around his throne, casting our crowns down at his feet (Revelation 4:10).

But we are not just waiting for a crown. We are already crowned. Our current crown isn't made with gold or diamonds, but with the steadfast love and tender mercies of our God (Psalm 103:4). The Lord himself has crowned us with the precious jewels of his character, his heart.

In the same way that a monarch's crown symbolises their relationship with their country and their subjects, so our crown speaks of our relationship with God. We have received and now daily enjoy his steadfast love and tender mercies. We are clothed in them. They sit on our heads, defining us – proclaiming who we are and *whose* we are. Like the coronation crown, the crowns on our heads reflect the status, honour, power and authority that have been given to us.

We have been saved and secured with loving-kindness and tender mercies. These crowns adorn our heads now that we have been brought into God's family. Isn't it wonderful that, as well as being rich, relentless and unrestrained, the mercy of God is also tender? He is compassionate towards us. His love for us is steadfast. He wants to do us good. He wants us as his own.

And as a sign that we belong to him, we are crowned with his tender mercies.

Unlike the St Edward's Crown, our crowns do not make an appearance only once or twice a century for a coronation. Unlike King Charles III, we do not wear our crowns temporarily. They do not just come out for momentous occasions. They sit permanently on our heads, immovable.

Crowned for a purpose

God crowns us for his glory and our good, which is incredible enough. But we are not crowned just for us. Like the precious St Edward's Crown, which sits high on the heads of kings and queens for all to see, our crown of steadfast love is meant to attract attention. As the dazzling diamonds of the Imperial State Crown reflect the light around them, our crowns of tender mercies are designed to reflect the light of God's mercy to the people he has placed in our lives. This crown may not be visible in the same way as crowns made of gold and gemstones, but it is supposed to be perceptible to those around us and draw them to the One who has crowned us – and who is willing to crown any that come to him.

Human crowns set apart the royal from the ordinary, the ruling from the ruled, the elite from the common. But the crown God bestows is available to all – anyone who will yield their heart to the King of kings, who humbly wore a crown of thorns so he could make a way for us to receive an imperishable crown of steadfast love and tender mercy that would be ours to wear forevermore.

We have become 'a royal priesthood'. Why? So that we 'may proclaim the excellencies of him who called [us] out of darkness into his marvellous light' (1 Peter 2:9). He has shown us mercy; not just for our own sakes, but to draw others to Jesus. As the apostle Paul writes: 'But for that very reason I was shown mercy so that in me, the worst of sinners, Christ Jesus might display his immense patience as an example for those who would believe in him and receive eternal life' (1 Timothy 1:16, NIV).

Our crowns proclaim who we are, but they display *his* glory, not *ours*. And his glory, as we have seen, is intrinsically bound up in his mercy, which we find to be extraordinary in its tenderness towards us. Merciful thinking dismantles the lie that my life is all about me. It reminds me that the purpose of my life is much higher and grander than that. When we think mercifully, we develop a powerful mix of humility (recognising that the world does not revolve around me) and purpose (a deep awareness that my life matters), which flies in the face of a culture that tells me I am the centre of my story but, conversely, that my life only matters if I make a mark that can be seen by others.

We were made for God. When we centre our lives on the One for whom we exist (1 Corinthians 8:6), we discover he has crowned us with tender mercies so that others will be drawn to him through us. Becoming a mercy-bringer first requires us to acknowledge that our lives are about Jesus – that our purpose is not to 'find ourselves' or achieve our own dreams, but to fix our eyes on him and to follow his will.

As we are transfixed by him, we are transformed by him. And as we make him, rather than ourselves, the centre of our lives, we grow in a confident assurance that he will work in and through us to display his splendour to those around us who desperately need his mercy.

19

Your life matters

Your life is not about you, but God has mercifully made the world in such a way that your life matters. You, as an individual, with all your weird and wonderful ways, matter. You were planned by the Father to be alive right now, at this point in history, for his glory and for the people around you. Some of us are acutely aware that our lives are not about us, because our pendulum sits at the other extreme, where we conclude that it doesn't make much difference whether we exist or not.

We can easily trundle along, living our mundane lives and believing the lie that only those who stand out matter. Our culture surreptitiously tells us that those who really count are the ones with popularity and prestige, fame and fortune, success and status. But God has made it so that even the most unremarkable person is made for impact. Our mundane lives matter.

I came through 2022 and 2023 with great joy. They were better years for me than any that had gone before. One of the main reasons was that nothing happened to me. There were no soaring highs or crushing lows. There were little highs and little lows, the everyday fluctuations of moods and work and relationships, the normal revelations and repentances that are par for the course for followers of Jesus. But there was no drama. Life bumbled along, and I bumbled along with it. It was glorious.

The preceding years had featured dramatic peaks and troughs – with a lot more of the latter than the former. I cannot recall many years of my life when something major hasn't happened, either within or around me, so it was the mercy of God to have two years of respite from the things that had gone before.

In the steadiness and stability of 2022 and 2023, I knew the tender hands of the Father moulding me into someone who, for the first time in my life, was becoming steady and stable too. This was not an overnight transformation or a sudden change, though it felt that way in some respects. I had been maturing and growing for several years, but only at this point were my deep roots revealed by visible results. Like Joseph, it became very clear that God had eventually 'made me fruitful in the land of my suffering' (Genesis 41:52, NIV).

In these uneventful years, I stopped being at the mercy of inner turmoil and outward circumstances – 'fighting without and fear within' (2 Corinthians 7:5) – and matured from being an expert in my miseries and an infant in God's mercies[1] into a woman anchored and astonished by those mercies.

I was markedly transformed in that unremarkable season.

Mercy in the mundane

God is at work just as much in the mundane as he is in the mountain and valley seasons. His mercies are new *every* morning, whether we are enjoying the best, the hardest or the blandest moments of our lives.

I had a friend who often expressed real concern about how mundane her life was. She looked at the lives of others and felt as though her day-to-day life was very underwhelming by comparison. Social media has compounded our ability to compare. Our lives shrink before our eyes as we look at our lowlights through the lens of other people's highlights. Holding up our troubles, grief and lack against the publicly curated lives of others is a ubiquitous form of self-harm.

Comparison is always unmerciful to someone.

But in the purposes of God, even the most mundane life is made for impact.

I have friends who have moved to the other side of the world on mission, prayed for the sick and seen miraculous healings, led multisite churches with hundreds of members, written books, preached on platforms, mixed with government leaders, influenced national policy and regularly appeared on TV. But the people who have had the most profound impact on my life have been those whose names you would not know – those who have walked faithfully alongside me or come into my life for a specific season, by the grace of God.

In fact, the friend most concerned about her mundane life shaped who I am today more than most other people I have met. Even though she was only meaningfully in my day-to-day life for a year or so, God worked through her to transform some of my deep-rooted issues and habits. This one self-proclaimed mundane person has, directly or indirectly, changed the majority of my daily routines: the time I get up, the time I go to bed, my prayer life. My reading, social media, eating, fasting and exercise habits have all changed significantly for the better as I imitated and learned from her disciplines. At the same time, some really bad habits were broken – some I was already aware of (such as the chronic habit of hitting snooze on my alarm clock) and some I didn't even know I had (such as fixating on certain thought patterns).

No matter how unremarkable we think our lives are, we were created to make a difference. We were created to bring glory to God and to be a blessing to the people around us, whether they are in our lives for five minutes or fifty years.

We are not world-changers

Not long after I committed my life to Jesus, the song 'History Maker' by Christian rock band Delirious? became an anthem for teenage Christians across the UK. Over a decade later it was rereleased and made it to number four in the UK's Official Singles Chart.[2] At the same time, the prevailing narrative in the church circles I was part of was that we were all destined to become international missionaries or world-changers. I grew into my faith, like many others around me, believing that if I didn't become famous for leading thousands of people to Jesus or overturning global injustices, I would have failed as a Christian.

But God has not called you or me to change the world. The vast majority of us are not, and will never be, history-makers, planet-shakers or world-changers. Even if we get to serve Jesus in ways we think are exciting, the reality of day-to-day life is that there is a lot more mundanity than exhilaration. And that's because it is all about Jesus, not us. We are not called to make a name for ourselves, but to bring glory to *his* name.

Some of us might end up doing things we dreamed of, but the danger there is that we find ourselves disappointed if the reality does not live up to expectations. When we long for anything over a period of time and then eventually attain it, it rarely fulfils in the way we hoped it would.

When I became Chief Executive of Jubilee+, I thought my days would be full of excitement as I cast vision, changed churches and influenced hearts. Some days it is a *bit* like that. But I definitely spend many more hours wading through emails, discussing budget lines and planning my diary than I'd imagined.

It is so easy for us to think that one day, when 'x' happens, every moment of every day will be caught up in an exciting faith adventure. But our lives simply aren't like that, and neither are the lives of the 'famous' Christians we celebrate.

I recently spoke to the youth in my church about George Müller. I talked about his extraordinary work in setting up and running five orphanages in Bristol during the nineteenth century, and about some of the incredible miracles of provision he saw, but that is not what I focused on. I told them that Müller did not pursue fame, but faith. I explained that he wasn't bothered about popularity, but about the power and provision of God.

Most of us are called to ordinary, even mundane, lives of simple service to Jesus in our local communities. But this doesn't mean we don't matter. On the contrary, God has ordained that our lives matter more than we can possibly understand. My 'mundane' friend, who helped me to form some good habits and break some bad ones, may never know the impact she has had on me, but I am significantly changed by the brief period in which our lives intersected.

We were not made to change the world, but we were made for impact. We were made to be changed and to bring change. We probably won't make history, but we can make a difference in the lives of those God has placed around us.

It can be hard to grasp how our lives are mundane yet still matter, because the world around us looks to status, achievements, talent and profile to decide how important we are. But irrespective of any of these things, in the purposes and mercies of God: 'You matter. I matter. It's the hardest thing in theology to believe.'[3]

God knows all the days of our lives. From the most exciting to the most boring, they are written in his book before one of them comes to pass (Psalm 139:16). However mundane our daily lives may feel to us, they matter.

Merciful thinking does not discount the impact I may have. That is false humility.

It is one of the great mercies of God that he has orchestrated it so that our lives count. We get to make a difference – to the people we love dearly, and even to those we come into contact with fleetingly. One of the best ways we can shape our thinking around this is to ask the Lord, as David did: 'Whom can I show your mercy to today?'

Part 4

MERCIFUL ACTIONS

Merciful thinking changes how we see ourselves and others. It humbles us with the knowledge that our lives are not about us, and it exalts us with the dignity that the One who made us says we matter. Hearts that truly love mercy can lay aside judgements, comparisons, and notions of being deserving and undeserving, to become 'vessels of mercy' towards others (Romans 9:23).

When our heart attitudes are gently and lovingly exposed by the Holy Spirit, revealing where we have taken on worldly thinking and failed to love mercy, the purpose is not just for us to repent (as vital as that is), but also that we will actively pursue lives characterised by mercy. God rises up to show us mercy (Isaiah 30:18, NIV) and wants us to rise up to show mercy to others.

When we cultivate merciful thoughts, we can be friends with people who are not like us. Those we once considered unworthy of mercy can become very precious, as we no longer divide people into categories of 'us and them' or 'deserving and undeserving'. Recognising the mercy we received while we were enemies of God, we are empowered to love our enemies and do good to those around us, regardless of how they treat us.

Mercy enables us to welcome people into our lives, churches and communities on the basis of God's mercy to us, not whether we feel they belong or know how to behave. And it moves us to tell people's stories with kindness and compassion, knowing that God has done the same for us.

Thinking mercifully frees us to embrace humility. It is no accident that Micah 6:8 locks mercy, justice and humility together. Mercy requires humility – a recognition that God does not owe me anything, and that each day of my life is an undeserved gift from the One who has not treated me as my sins deserved (Psalm 103:10, NIV). And humility leads to mercy as we soberly judge ourselves; not thinking of ourselves more highly than we should, but considering others as more significant and looking to their interests (Romans 12:3; Philippians 2:3-4).

Mercy is not soft, but it is gentle, and as we renew our minds and become more merciful in our thinking, we will grow in gentleness. Our harsh edges are refined and our hard attitudes are purified. We drop our stones of condemnation, because we are very conscious of the One who knows our sin but cast not a single stone in our direction.

Merciful thinking turns into merciful actions because we want to express something of the mercy we have received. Over time, as we give ourselves to loving mercy, our feelings of hostility towards others are replaced by feelings of compassion, and acts of kindness become the natural overflow of our grateful hearts.

The Father wants to take us on a journey that begins with marvelling in wonder at the mercy he has shown us. We start there, but we do not stay there. The more precious and profound our understanding of the mercy we have received, the more our thinking will change. As our minds are renewed, our hearts will start to truly love mercy.

But there is a next, and vital, step on this journey, which brings us into our true identity as children of God; not just bearing his image, not just carrying his name, but also bringing his mercy.

Delighting in the mercy we have received is the doorway to delighting that we are called to be merciful, just as our Father is merciful – that we get to imitate our Father and be conformed to the image of Christ, our older brother (Romans 8:29; Hebrews 2:11; Mark 3:34–35).

In a world that desperately lacks mercy, followers of Jesus are called to be an army of mercy-bringers.

20

Do mercy

Immersing ourselves in the mercy of God should cause us to worship him, to see signs of it everywhere (even in the hardest times and experiences in our lives), and to have our hearts changed so that we love mercy and think mercifully. But the call on our lives is higher and broader than that. We are to become like Jesus by *doing* mercy.

Given that Jesus is 'the radiance of God's glory and the exact representation' (Hebrews 1:3, NIV) of God the Father, it comes as no surprise that he started his earthly ministry by reading a manifesto of mercy.

Following his temptation in the wilderness, Jesus returned full of the Holy Spirit and began to teach in Jewish synagogues. When he came to Nazareth, to the synagogue of his childhood, the scroll of Isaiah was handed to him. He was not told which bit to read, and he did not pick the words at random, wherever his finger landed in the text. No. He deliberately 'found the place where it was written' (Luke 4:17) – the specific part he wanted to read aloud. Jesus launched his public ministry by revealing that he had come for those in poverty, captivity and oppression.

Jesus often said: 'The kingdom of God has come near' (for example in Mark 1:15). In reading from what we now know as Isaiah 61, Jesus revealed glimpses of what it meant for him to usher in the kingdom of God. When Jesus came, there was an invasion of heaven to earth. Often when that sort of language is used, we think of signs and wonders, of miracles and healing. And those are definitely part of what it means for the kingdom of God to be rolled out on the earth.

But often we fail to remember that a key aspect of the kingdom coming – of God's will being done on earth as it is in heaven – is that the gospel is good news for those who are trapped in poverty of various kinds. Jesus was anointed not just to meet people at their point of crisis, though he absolutely did that. He was also anointed by the Spirit to lift people up out of their poverty. And so are we. It is a vital part of bringing the kingdom of God to those around us, as we shall see in a later chapter.

Jesus came to reveal the Father to us. That is why, when we pay close attention to the Gospels, we see that mercy is not just in Jesus' opening manifesto, but everywhere.

We find it in the stories Jesus told. In the Parable of the Good Samaritan, Jesus helps the expert in the law to see that loving our neighbour is about practical demonstrations of a mercy that transcends barriers. The road from Jerusalem to Jericho was a steep descent of about seventeen miles, some of which ran through rocky desert territory. It is interesting that Jesus makes a point of mentioning this, but does not comment on the fact that the man should have known better than to walk a route that was notoriously dangerous for lone travellers. If his bad decision played a part in what happened to him, Jesus does not say so. He just tells us that 'he fell among robbers, who stripped him and beat him' (Luke 10:30). A priest and a Levite saw him lying half-dead and passed by, not wanting to get involved. But a Samaritan 'had compassion' (Luke 10:33) and came to his aid.

After telling the story, Jesus asked the expert in the law which of the three men was a neighbour to the beaten man. He answered: 'The one who had mercy on him.'

Jesus replied, 'Go and do likewise' (Luke 10:37, NIV).

'Do' is the operative word here. We have already seen that Jesus wants his followers to be merciful – to be characterised by mercy – and here we see his emphasis on our actions. Jesus wants us to *do* mercy.

Being merciful does not just make us think differently, tweet differently and talk differently. It makes us *do* differently.

Imitating Jesus

Jesus made it clear that there is a direct correlation between our merciful actions towards others and the way we treat him. I sometimes read passages of Scripture such as the Parable of the Sheep and the Goats (Matthew 25:31–45) really quickly – eager to skip to the parts of the Bible I find more palatable. But that is a dangerous thing to do, because here we find a merciful warning from Jesus to his disciples in private[1] that we would do well to heed. He said plainly that when we show mercy by providing for the hungry and thirsty, clothing those in need, visiting people in prison and inviting strangers in, we are showing that we know and belong to him.

Some believe this parable only applies to the way we treat other Christians, but from the inclusion of 'strangers' (the Greek word *xenos*, meaning foreigner, is used in Ephesians 2:12 and 19 to describe us before we placed our faith in Christ), I don't think that Jesus was talking exclusively about other believers. Either way, he takes personally our practical acts of mercy towards others. This is sobering: if we belong to Jesus, we will take these words seriously and act mercifully towards those in need.

From his inner circle of disciples to religious leaders who were trying to catch him out, Jesus continually challenged his listeners to be merciful. Some of the stories of mercy Jesus told would have provoked uproar. I mentioned in an earlier chapter that when I read about the vineyard owner who paid everyone equally, whether they worked all day or just one hour, I feel a little indignant. It doesn't seem fair. Yet Jesus makes the point that the owner is free to be as merciful and generous as he wishes, and no one has the right to resent it (Matthew 20:1–16).

In fact, Jesus calls us to be similarly generous. For example, when telling parables about banquets, he says we should invite people that others would not invite – people who cannot repay us (Luke 14:12–24).

Jesus outlined what mercy looks like, but he came not just to talk, but to act mercifully. He lived it out. Many of the parables Jesus told were stories of mercy in action, and he powerfully demonstrated what a heart of mercy looks like in practice by the way he treated people.

There are lots of little touches of Jesus' mercy in the Gospel accounts that we can easily miss if we are not paying close attention. For example, when he meets a man who was born blind and the disciples assume it is because of his or his parents' sin, Jesus tells them things are not that black and white (John 9). This is an odd story in many ways. Imagine seeing Jesus mix his spit with mud and put it on the man's eyes! The man has never seen anything in his entire life, and then suddenly he sees. It must have been extraordinary to watch this unfold.

But the mercy of Jesus is not only present for this man at the time of the healing miracle. We see it at work afterwards, too. Having received his sight, the man born blind would have lost his community, as he would not have been able to return to his life of begging with others who were sick, injured or disabled. Instead of being welcomed by the religious leaders, he was cast out of the synagogue, and his own parents preferred to let that happen than to speak up on his behalf and risk being excommunicated themselves.

He gained his sight but had no one to rejoice with. Isn't it wonderful that when Jesus heard that the man had been cast out, he tracked him down? Healing the man was a powerful act of mercy, but Jesus extended his mercy yet further by going to find the man so he could offer him eternal life (John 9:35–38).

Again, we return to this biblical theme of actively looking to show mercy. Jesus went the extra mile (Matthew 5:41). Do we? I find that I am often satisfied with doing the minimum required. Sometimes I am content to do just enough to feel good about myself, but can easily resist pushing myself to look for ways to be more merciful. I might donate soup to my local food bank, but stop short of volunteering. Or I might do some shifts there, but never contemplate inviting someone to dinner. We have developed many ways to show crumbs of compassion and ease our consciences while maintaining the same level of personal comfort. Jesus calls us to be merciful at the core of who we are, and to do mercy in the ways he demonstrated.

Jesus went looking for the man who had been cast out so he could draw him in. The apostle Paul tells us that Jesus has extended this same mercy to us. I wonder if there are any sweeter words in the Bible than the seven Paul uses in his letter to the Christians in Philippi: 'Christ Jesus has made me his own' (Philippians 3:12).

Like the man born blind, Jesus has tracked us down and pursued us so he can show us his extraordinary mercy. Heeding the words of Jesus in his parables should cause us to take stock. But seeing the mercy of Jesus in action should cause our hearts to soar in worship that propels us to: 'Go and do likewise!'

21
The bias of mercy

'Doing mercy' means caring about the physical needs of those around us. It is not limited to that, but we cannot claim to be merciful while remaining unmoved by poverty. The Good Samaritan did not just *feel* compassion, he *demonstrated* it. His feelings turned into practical, generous provision. Likewise, in the Parable of the Sheep and the Goats, Jesus talks about tangible acts of mercy through which the needs of the hungry, thirsty, naked, strangers, sick and imprisoned are met.

If God's mercy has a bias towards anyone, it is to those in poverty. Those facing need seem to attract his special attention. Time and again we read that God is displeased with his own people because of how they treat those in hardship around them. The Lord frequently expresses anger towards his people when they are heartless towards those in need, neglecting or even exploiting them.

A whistle-stop tour through the Bible shows us that, throughout human history, God has been especially concerned about those who are vulnerable. He cares deeply about the plight of those trapped in poverty or oppressed by injustice. There are literally hundreds of verses about poverty and justice that back this up, yet we can easily miss the fact that God's mercy is especially focused on those in poverty. And if we miss it, we miss its application for us, and a crucial element of Jesus' call to us to 'be merciful' like our Father.

Old Testament provision

One example of how easily we can miss this is in the Old Testament narratives. In Genesis, we so often read and tell Joseph's story as a story of God's faithfulness, of Joseph's faithfulness, and of God's purposes and plans. All of this is good and helpful, but it's not the whole story. Perhaps one of the most frequently quoted verses is when Joseph tells his brothers that what they meant for evil, God intended for good (Genesis 50:20). But so often when we quote this or hear it quoted, we stop short of mentioning the good that God intended: 'so that you... do not come to poverty' (Genesis 45:11).

Joseph knew God had sent him ahead to Egypt so that the famine would not plunge his people into poverty and destroy their lives (Genesis 45:4–8). The Lord was concerned about their physical needs and basic survival. And not just theirs. In saving them, many Egyptians were also saved – even though God knew they would later forget all about Joseph, and would oppress and enslave the Israelites. He had mercy on them, sparing them from the famine even though he knew they wouldn't turn to him.

We can just as easily miss God's heart when we read about the law of Moses, even though his mercy towards the poorest is woven throughout it. Looking through the lens of our individualistic culture, we can be fooled into thinking that the law is just rules about personal morality. But it extends far beyond that – it is also God laying out for his people the best way for their society (and all societies) to flourish.

When God was setting out how his people should live, we see him identifying very clearly the needs of those in poverty. He made numerous stipulations for the protection of, and provision for, those in need. For example, gleaning. This was to counter the intuition of farmers who, when gathering their crops, would naturally go back to pick up anything that had fallen by the wayside. Left to their own devices, they would make sure they picked up every last grain so they could feed their families and sell what remained to others in the community. This is not wrong; it is practical.

But God wants his people to be merciful – to be different, distinct, set apart from those around them – so he tells them not to do this. Instead, he instructs them to leave whatever fell when they gathered so it could be picked up by those who were in poverty and didn't have the means to gather or buy their own food (Leviticus 19:9–10, 23:22). Ruth, the great-grandmother of King David and ancestor of Jesus, benefited from this mercy built into the law when she gleaned in Boaz's field (Ruth 2).

God also commands that wages should be paid immediately and not deferred (Deuteronomy 24:14–15); interest shouldn't be charged on loans, so people cannot be exploited in their hour of need (Exodus 22:25–26); tithes are not just for priests but also for those in poverty (Deuteronomy 14:28–29); and even that profit shouldn't be made on food (Leviticus 25:37). Think how different our society would be if we all lived like this! Not just society, but also the Church. There is a clear challenge in the law for us to make sure that we are channelling a significant amount of our income into alleviating poverty. Tithes are typically thought of as ten per cent, but in Acts 4:34–35 it seems that all the money laid at the apostles' feet was used to support those in need. Some of our churches struggle to commit ten per cent to poverty relief. Imagine what it would look like if we imitated the early Church and gave it all!

There were two specific provisions in law that particularly demonstrated God's mercy towards those in poverty. The first is the Sabbath year – the seventh year – when debts were cancelled (Deuteronomy 15:1–2). The second was the Year of Jubilee, which came around every fifty years and required not only that debts be cancelled, but also that land would be returned to its original owners, and that those who had put themselves into servitude or slavery (which happened in those times owing to poverty) would be released (Leviticus 25).

The whole economic system was built on mercy. No debt was forever. The extremes of wealth and poverty were modified. The rich couldn't simply get richer and richer at the expense of others, and there was always hope for those in poverty, because God had instituted these two key moments of reset for his people.

His mercy towards those who had fallen on hard times went even further. It wasn't just a reset to zero, where they were sent on their way with nothing but the hope that they might have better luck this time. Yes, those in poverty regained their freedom and their land, and had their debts cancelled, but they also gained what they needed for a fresh start, because God said to those who were doing well for themselves: 'And when you release them, do not send them away empty-handed. Supply them liberally from your flock, your threshing-floor and your winepress' (Deuteronomy 15:13–14, NIV). As well as release and reset, they were given *a liberal supply* of all they needed, so they had the best chance of flourishing.

That God gives us another chance is an incredible expression of his mercy and kindness towards us, but it goes further than just cancelling our debts and letting us walk free from them – though that would be wonderful in and of itself. On top of this, he gives us all we need to live in the good of our newfound freedom, both economically and spiritually. He is merciful towards us in all aspects of our poverty.

Past and future blessings

Throughout the law of Moses, God repeats two clear reasons why his people should be merciful to those in need. First, because of God's *past* blessings towards us. He has shown us compassion so we can show compassion to others; he has blessed us so we can bless others; he has shown us mercy so we can be merciful (Deuteronomy 15:14). We *can* in the sense that we have the ability to do so, because he has modelled it for us and empowered us to follow his example. And we *can* in the sense that we have the opportunity to do so, because he has called us to specific deeds of mercy and will bring specific people across our path so we have numerous occasions to put our merciful hearts into action.

Our past blessings from God include redemption from slavery (Deuteronomy 15:15, 24:18, 22). We may not have been literal slaves, like the Israelites, but we were slaves to sin and death, to the kingdom of darkness and to the one who rules it. Like the Israelites, we know what it is to be set free from a tyrannical slavemaster who has no concern for our welfare. And as those who remember what it felt like to be enslaved, we now get to be bringers of mercy, hope and freedom to those who are labouring under one form of oppression or another.

Second, because of God's *future* blessings for us. He promises to bless us when we show mercy in the ways he has set out for us. In multiple verses in Deuteronomy (for example 14:29, 15:6, 10, 18, 24:19), he says he will bless the work of our hands when we meet the needs of those in poverty. (We will explore more about the promises of God in relation to how we treat others at the end of Part 4.)

But there is also a very significant third reason why God set mercy into the heart of the law of Moses. Part of God's plan for how his people would be set apart and noticeably different from everyone around them was, and is, that there should be no one in poverty among them. The outworking of a people characterised by mercy is the absence of poverty. In Deuteronomy 15:4–5, God makes it plain: 'There need be no poor people among you, for in the land the LORD your God is giving you to possess as your inheritance, he will richly bless you, if only you fully obey the LORD your God and are careful to follow all these commands I am giving you today.'

If the people of God fully obey the commands of God, mercy will flow so abundantly between them that there will not be a single person in need among them. This might sound impossible, but it is exactly what we see in the book of Acts. Jesus had died, risen and ascended, and his followers had just experienced baptism in the

Holy Spirit. There had been an outbreak of salvation and the early Church was beginning to take shape.

What the Israelites were unable to achieve in their society because they had not obeyed the commands of God, the disciples were now fully empowered by the Spirit to realise in their community. 'There was not a needy person among them' (Acts 4:34) because each person had adopted an attitude of mercy, sharing what they had, even selling what they owned, so that no one in the fellowship of believers would suffer lack.

This is particularly extraordinary because sociologists and historians tell us that in any Greek or Roman city in those days, approximately fifty per cent of the population would have lived in poverty or on the cusp of it. Imagine what it would have been like to live in that environment, where half the people around you are in need, yet not a single person in the Church lacked the essentials. No doubt it would have pointed people towards the merciful God, who calls us to show mercy to those around us, and especially to those in poverty, so much so that we stand in stark contrast to the communities around us. Wouldn't that cause people to wonder about the God we serve?[1]

There is a challenge here for local churches, and for us as individual Christians, to not tolerate poverty in our midst. No one among us should be in need. As each follower of Jesus responds to the call to be merciful and actively seeks to put that mercy into action, we must share what we have and meet the needs of others. First, we must eradicate poverty in the Church. Then, our generosity to those who are facing hardship must overflow, spilling out into the community around us.

Doing mercy looks like sharing what we have – our time, skills, money, possessions and power – with those who have less.

22
Sharing power

It is not just in the Old Testament law that we see God's mercy directed towards the poorest and most vulnerable. We could take a tour through the writings of the major and minor prophets to find it writ large. It is spread throughout the psalms, proverbs and historical narratives. It is unmissable in the Gospels and Acts of the Apostles, and it is scattered across the letters of Paul, Peter, James and John.

While the mercy of God is biased towards those afflicted by poverty or injustice, it is not exclusively theirs. To our polarised society, perhaps one of the most scandalous aspects of the good news of Jesus Christ is that no one is beyond the reach of his mercy. Our culture tends to pit people against one another. For the majority who live in the middle rather than at the extremes of wealth and poverty, privilege and lack, strength and weakness, we are taught to blame both the haves and the have-nots. We are told, for example, that poverty is simultaneously the fault of the lazy scroungers who just need to work harder and the powerful decision-makers who have no compassion because everything fell into their laps.

The snobbery of the elite who look down their noses at the downtrodden is matched blow for blow by the reverse snobbery of the lowly who glare with disgust at the corruption, hubris and ignorant bliss of those who had everything handed to them on a silver platter. One group is in want because they did not apply themselves well enough to earn what they need; the other group enjoys a birthright of riches and opportunities they did not have to earn. What both groups have in common is a self-righteousness that denigrates the other: one group is too irresponsible to be

trusted to know what is best for them; the other is too privileged to understand what life is really like for the masses.

Jesus dignifies neither argument and refuses to take sides. He offers mercy to all who are despised, irrespective of who is doing the despising.

The gospel is good news to the poor, but it is not the preserve of the poor.

Jesus sought out the marginalised and disadvantaged, but he also pursued the rich and powerful with mercy. In fact, Jesus affirms and upsets both groups, drawing to himself the powerless and the powerful, the oppressed and the oppressor. As Christopher Watkin says, Jesus did not just reach out to those 'we might call "fashionable" marginalised groups, those that bring kudos and social capital to those seen to be helping them… The net of Jesus' compassion is spread more widely than most of the marginalised groups on our cultural radar today.'[1]

Being merciful will affect how we treat the elite, as well as those who have nothing by which to commend themselves to us, because doing mercy dispossesses us of our hard-hearted attitudes towards those who are not like us. This means we can show kindness to all, assuming the best, and speaking and acting accordingly.

Mercy in action recognises that no 'side' is all good or all bad. One practical outworking of this can be seen in political life. I worked for a parliamentary candidate in the run-up to the UK's 2015 General Election. I really wanted her to win – I had confidence that she would be a committed public servant, fighting for the rights of those on the margins. She represented many of the values I hold dear. But the night before polling stations opened, I sat next to a guy in my church who was working for the opposition candidate, and we prayed together for God's blessing on our political opponents, their families and their teams. When it came to the outcome, we prayed only for God's will.

his behalf. But part of the Father's mercy is that he catches us up in his plans and purposes. This is true for all of us in Christ. God has prepared work for us to do in co-labouring with Jesus (John 14:12; Ephesians 2:10; 1 Corinthians 3:9).

But God's power-sharing is more radical than we might imagine, because he specifically raises up the unexpected – the weak, vulnerable, poverty-stricken, grieving, broken-hearted and oppressed – to participate in his merciful work of renewing and restoring others.

Consolidating our power base and reaching for more is the way of the world.

Laying down power for the good of others is the way of the cross.

God's mercy does not just change our lives, as wonderful as that is, but it transforms us into agents of change. The mercy of God turns us into conduits of God's mercy towards others. We are lifted out of our brokenness so that we can raise others up. This means we can expect to be a blessing to those around us; not just individuals we come into contact with, but our communities as a whole.

I grew up in relative poverty in the deprived coastal town of Hastings, which was once called 'Hell-on-Sea' by the *Daily Mail*.[2] Other headlines about my hometown have included 'The Lost Resort', 'Suicide Black Spot' and 'Sad Symbol of Decline into Crime'.

Since those newspaper reports from the late 1990s, £680 million has been invested in Hastings to try to improve it for those who live here but, as Sky News depressingly reports, this money has had 'no tangible effect'.[3] Despite all the government money poured into Hastings over the last twenty-five years, the town still suffers from inadequate housing, limited healthcare, poor infrastructure and comparatively low life expectancy. When I read Isaiah prophesying about 'places long devastated', places that have been 'devastated for generations' (Isaiah 61:4, NIV), Hastings fits the bill.

But the promise of God through the prophet Isaiah is that people like me – those who were once in poverty themselves – are raised up

My candidate lost. I sat on the beach at 5 a.m. feeling gutted, having been up all night awaiting the results. But God reminded me over the following weeks and months that, because I know his mercy and am called to be a mercy-bringer, I am not permitted to vilify my opponents. I can disagree – even vehemently – and campaign against policies I feel are unjust or unfair. But mercy does not allow me to tear down another person. As one of my friends says: 'When we argue, one of our goals should be to leave the other person intact.' In an increasingly polarised society, that is countercultural mercy.

Merciful and mighty

The way Jesus engages with power goes beyond reaching out to the powerful. Jesus was the most powerful person who ever lived, and he consistently channelled this power into his great delight: showing mercy.

We don't often think about the power and mercy of God being intricately connected. Power conjures up images of strength and might, whereas mercy seems to lean towards meekness and humility. But the mercy of God is also powerful, and is often demonstrated in powerful ways.

In the same way that the glory of God is revealed in the mercy of God, so we see that every powerful act Jesus performs is actually, at its root, an act of mercy.

Jesus' first miracle – turning water into wine at a wedding feast (John 2:1–11) – was a supernatural act that demonstrated his power, but it was also an incredible act of mercy. It would have been far more shameful than we can perhaps comprehend, in our modern Western world, for the wine to run dry at a wedding. Even though he tells his mother it is not yet time for him to reveal who he is, Jesus performs this miracle to spare the bridegroom's shame.

When Jesus fed the multitudes, we are told it was because they were hungry and he had compassion on them, not wanting to send them away in case they passed out for lack of food (Mark 8:1–9; Matthew 15:32). He had mercy on them. He could have whittled down the numbers by weeding out those who had been around him long enough to know that they should have brought food with them. He could have been selective about feeding only those who really needed his help. He could have told the disciples to check who had the means to sort themselves out. He could have examined the motives of their hearts and separated out those who had real faith and wanted to respond to his teachings from those who were just there to see a miracle and had no real interest in following him. But he didn't do any of these things. He worked wonders with little, feeding them all – not to show off his supernatural power, but because they were hungry and he is merciful.

When Jesus told the storm to pipe down, and the wind and waves obeyed him, settling immediately into 'a great calm' (Matthew 8:23–27), the disciples marvelled at his incredible power. But Jesus did not still the storm simply as a display of his might. He did it as an act of mercy, because the disciples were afraid. The boat was never going to sink. The disciples were never going to drown. He could have just told them to have more faith, or that this wasn't how they or he would die. He performed the miracle not to calm the storm but to calm their fears. Yes, it displayed his power and authority, but it was also an act of mercy that brought peace to the water, and more importantly to their hearts.

When Jesus raised the dead, it was because he had compassion on the grieving. He tenderly said to the widow who had also lost her only child: 'Do not weep,' before mercifully restoring the son to life and giving him back to his mother (Luke 7:11–15). Setting free those who were demonised was another display of his power and authority that was deeply rooted in his mercy. That is how Jesus himself describes it when he says to the man living in the tombs at Gerasenes: 'Go home to your friends and tell them how much the Lord has done for you, and how he has had mercy on you' (Mark 5:19).

Often when we read about Jesus healing the sick, we are told that he was moved by compassion. What's more, we see that Jesus healed regardless of whether or not he was thanked (Luke 17:11–16). He had mercy on all who cried out to him in distress. He was merciful, just as his Father is merciful.

Jesus used his power to show mercy, and so can we. We can and should pray for the people around us to experience God's supernatural mercy, whether that be for provision of their needs or healing of their bodies, minds or hearts. We can also use the power we hold in our spheres of influence – whether that be teaching the children in our lives that growing in mercy, compassion, kindness and generosity is part of following Jesus, or building relationships with those who make decisions that affect our communities. Perhaps you have responsibility and authority in your workplace and can spend some time thinking about what it would mean to use your power there to show mercy to others.

Working with God

One of the most merciful things Jesus did with his power was share it. In many of the miracles mentioned above, He did not work alone. Before turning water into wine, servants were invited to fill the jars. When feeding the multitudes, Jesus first asked the disciples to feed them, and when they couldn't, he involved them in organising the crowd, distributing the food and collecting leftovers. He also sent out seventy-two disciples to heal the sick (Luke 10:1–9).

Sharing his power by inviting us to participate in his work is something God has always done. In the garden of Eden, Adam was given the privilege of naming the animals, and even after the Fall, God continued to invite men and women to participate in his work on earth. The Lord did not need Noah to build a boat, or Moses and Esther to rescue the Israelites, or Deborah to bring wise judgements, or Isaiah, Micah, Amos and others to communicate on

by God so they can play a part in restoring the deprived communities that others might have written off. When I became a Christian, God lifted me out of poverty and changed my circumstances. I would have been happy with that, but his vision for me is far grander and his transformation in me is far deeper. I am maturing into an oak of righteousness that displays his splendour as I get involved in rebuilding, restoring and renewing others around me.

His mercy towards me is not just about me. In his mercy, I get to do good to others too. God grabbed hold of my life and turned it around in an instant, but his sanctifying work takes place slowly. Where I am impatient, he is merciful in his gradual and thorough surgery on my heart. I was so encouraged to learn that oak trees can take up to a century to mature. Even the fastest-growing oaks take twenty years. We need to be patient and merciful with ourselves, and with others, as we grow almost imperceptibly into the mighty oaks God has called us to be. But we also need to have God's big vision for people, no matter how far from it they seem to be.

Whatever power we have, we are to use it mercifully, and one of the most radical demonstrations of that is not just to help people at their point of need (as vital as that is), but to give away our power so that people who once depended on us to thrive (and maybe even survive), no longer need us. Doing mercy is often associated with developing a Saviour complex. It is easily done. Helping people feels good. The sense of being needed can be addictive.

But being merciful is not about *hoarding* power, as the world tries to do, but *sharing* it, especially with those who have none. It requires us to crucify our insecurities and fear of others no longer needing us, or even surpassing us. God's vision is that we will become mature oaks, deeply rooted; able to stand strong and to display his splendour. Mercy in action looks like coming alongside people when they need our support, giving them space to thrive, and letting them outgrow us as they become those who lift others up – showing them the same mercy they have been shown.

23

Merciful with money

My church leader once challenged me to go through my bank statements and take stock of how much money I was spending on luxuries compared with essentials. I was about to preach on materialism, and he pushed me to check myself as part of my preparation. At the time, I thought of myself as relatively generous. I'd certainly grown in generosity over my first couple of decades as a Christian. Tithing my income to the church had been a long-established habit, so much so that I barely thought about it. Increasingly, I had also felt moved by the Holy Spirit to be generous in various contexts, from giving to strangers, donating to charity, sponsoring friends, and even setting aside a small amount every month with the express purpose of giving it away as and when a need presented itself.

So as I approached the task of reviewing my outgoings, I imagined I would emerge from the exercise feeling pretty good about myself.

I was wrong.

Even though I was kind to myself in what I categorised as 'essential', I still came out spending between a quarter and a third of my income on luxuries each month.

I reasoned with myself. *That's not too bad. Don't be hard on yourself.* And one my friends said: 'I'm sure God wants you to have nice things.'

Maybe he does, but I'm not sure about that – it sounds like something the world around me would say. Either way, I'm pretty certain God is more interested in my being merciful with my money than spending it on things I don't need.

Money can be a great vehicle for showing mercy to people, but it can also be a huge obstacle. We live in a massively materialistic society, where the unspoken motto is: 'What's mine is mine.' If I worked hard for what I have, then it's fine to amass more and more, right?

In our culture it is now so common for us to spend money that isn't ours that we barely think about using credit cards to buy not just what we need, but what we want and cannot afford.[1]

Invest in mercy

The pursuit of money and possessions is rife, and Christians are not immune from it. It can be an uncomfortable topic of conversation, but if we are going to become people of mercy, we need to talk about what we do with our money and our stuff. Jesus is very clear that worrying about our possessions – even the essentials – is a pagan pursuit (Matthew 6:32, NIV). In fact, he told his disciples (which includes us!) to be so radically unconcerned about our own needs that we pursue treasure in heaven by selling our possessions and giving to those in need (Luke 12:13–34).

Are we willing to let the Holy Spirit nudge and convict us on this? I know I can be quite wedded to my own comfort. And if the apostle Paul felt the need to warn his spiritual son, Timothy, to flee from the love of money and craving for wealth (1 Timothy 6:6–11), it seems reasonable to assume that we need to watch ourselves here, too.

If we really pursue God's heart of mercy towards those around us, it will affect our wallets and our bank balances – and not just in small ways that let us feel good about ourselves without really costing us anything.

The way we use our money is one of the markers of how well we have understood the gospel. If we have received the good news as a consumer product, we are likely to enjoy its benefits to us rather than living it out.

The way John Wesley, one of the great preachers of the eighteenth century, handled his money is deeply challenging. He felt moved by God to see how much of his income he could give away to those in poverty. When he was twenty-eight, he earned £30 a year. He kept the £28 he needed to live on and gave away the remaining £2.

The next year, his income doubled but he saw no need for his expenditure to follow suit, so he still kept £28, this time giving away the £32 that was left. His income rose significantly the following year. He earned £90 and gave away £62. The highest amount Wesley earned in a single year was £1,400. Still he kept only what he needed to live on – this time £30 – and gave away the rest to those in need.

Challenging, isn't it? How many of us, under similar circumstances, choose to adjust our lifestyle instead of ploughing our excess income into mercy?

It is so easily done. In both my childhood and adult life, I have known times of financial hardship. I have been in overwhelming debt to the extent that a solicitor advised me to declare myself bankrupt. I slept on the floor for eighteen months because I didn't have a bed. But today I am Chief Executive of a national charity, with a salary that is comparatively modest but nevertheless provides me with a higher and more stable income than I ever imagined earning. I have known what it is to have very little, but I now know what it is to have more than enough. And in my experience, the transition from gratitude for the small things to taking most things for granted is swift and thorough, if it is allowed to go unchecked.

I can easily persuade myself that adjusting my lifestyle according to my increasing income is not a bad thing. After all, it's what we all do. It's normal. And worldly wisdom would tell me to save as much as I can so I don't have to worry about unforeseen circumstances. But I often feel the gentle prod of the Holy Spirit causing me to ask myself: *Is it ever OK for me to have way more than I need when people around me do not have the basics?*

If God's answer is 'No' – as I suspect it is – then I am called to be *more merciful* with my money… and *merciful* with *more* of my money. This makes me uncomfortable.

Overflowing generosity

In one of my previous books, I told the story of God asking me to lend someone the money to pay off their credit card debt, and of me initially saying no to God a few times – until I felt that he had backed me into a corner and I had no choice.[2] I wanted to pray for the person and for God to provide. God wanted me to share what I had in the bank.

I love hearing stories about someone having a very specific financial need, and God providing the exact amount through an unexpected tax rebate or cash posted anonymously through a letterbox. But I was not so keen when I asked the person at church how much debt they were in, and the figure they said was very close to the amount I had in my savings account at the time! The truth is, I am more comfortable being like the prodigal, receiving the lavish generosity of the father, than being prompted by God to imitate his mercy when it is costly.

But that is so often how God provides for people in need – through us, through his Church. Christians do not have the monopoly on generosity, but if we live up to our calling we will go far beyond common generosity, which gives out of our excess. The early Church lived in a completely different way from the society around them, with the believers 'selling their possessions and belongings and distributing the proceeds to all, as any had need' (Acts 2:45). This kind of merciful generosity pointed people to Jesus back then, and it still does now. It is a radically countercultural heart posture that says: 'What's mine is not just mine. No matter how hard I worked for it and feel I earned it, it is not all for me. It is yours, too. God has given it to me not just for my good, but for the good of others.'

It is not based on how much or how little we have. It wasn't only the rich young ruler Jesus told to 'sell all that you have and distribute to the poor' (Luke 18:22) – he said something very similar to the disciples. They would have had a lot less than the rich man, yet in the context of telling them not to be anxious about material things, Jesus said: 'Sell your possessions, and give to the needy' (Luke 12:33).

Our generosity and willingness to share does not start with our bank balance.

It starts with our heart attitudes.

The Christians in Macedonia had two things – an abundance of joy and extreme poverty – and when these two things were added together, they 'overflowed in a wealth of generosity' (2 Corinthians 8:2). The apostle Paul writes that they gave not *according* to their means, but *beyond* their means. That doesn't sound wise to me!

Biblical generosity is not based on our finances, but on our faith. In the past I would have counselled people against giving beyond their means, but the Macedonian Christians begged earnestly for the opportunity to give to others (2 Corinthians 8:1–5). If I were to beg earnestly for anything to do with my money, I would be more likely to beg earnestly for God to let me keep what I have, not to give it away!

This Macedonian mindset does not develop on its own. Being merciful with our money requires us to actively cultivate an attitude of generosity.

24

Merciful with stuff

A few years ago, a friend told me that he opened his wardrobe one day and realised he had a problem. He noticed how many branded items of clothing he had hanging up, including dozens of T-shirts he had rarely or never worn. Then he started thinking about how much he had spent on pairs of trainers.

As he contemplated his vast array of branded footwear and clothing, my friend felt the gentle conviction of the Holy Spirit and realised that materialism – this 'stuff' – had a grip on his heart. When he asked God what he should do about it, he felt he should only buy things if he could afford to buy two: one for himself and one to give away.

For a whole year, he applied this to everything he bought. If he picked up a cup of coffee on his way to work, he would buy one for someone else – blessing either a stranger in the queue behind him, or a colleague or friend. When he bought a cinema ticket, the same principle applied. When he visited a supermarket to shop for food, he purchased two of everything.

That year was the first in a long while that he did not spend upwards of £200 on a pair of trainers! By the end of it, the hold of money and possessions had been broken, and my friend had been more merciful with his money than ever before. More importantly, a lifestyle of giving away was embedded in his heart.

A tight grip

I really enjoy speaking and teaching on Acts 2 and Acts 4, where the first Christians sold what they had so there would be no one in need among them. I love the idea of that countercultural living we looked at in the last chapter, where instead of going along with the world's view of money and belongings, we resolve to have open hands.

But if I'm honest, I find it easier to bless someone by giving them money or buying something for them than sharing what I already own. Funnily enough, I find that God gives me ample opportunities to work on this! Bizarrely, I find it easier to share some of the bigger things I own. For example, a friend I used to work with at my local church often asked to borrow my car during the day. My church role did not often require me to leave the building, but he frequently needed to make pastoral visits. After the first couple of times of lending him my car, it became really easy to say yes. Even though he always joked when he returned that he had spent the last couple of hours doing handbrake turns in a field, I didn't have an inner tussle about him borrowing my car, because I knew he would return it.

Not so with smaller items. On many occasions I have stomped around my church building trying to hunt down whoever has 'borrowed' my phone charger without asking. On one occasion, a friend from church followed me around as I went from colleague to colleague, asking (or, more accurately, accusing) them about it. After about fifteen minutes, during which I became increasingly agitated, my friend put her hand on my arm to make me stand still, before saying, gently but firmly: 'Don't you preach about sharing, Nat?'

Gah!

I kept this in my head, but I wanted to yell: 'Sssssshhhhhhhh!'

She had graciously but clearly called me out!

The truth is, I don't want to share my phone charger because it's not likely to be returned, and it's clearly very precious to me. I guess something similar is at work when I finish each day at my desk by locking my mug away in a drawer so no one else can use it.

I have a friend whose reluctance to share is even more ridiculous than mine (which is handy when I want to feel better about myself!). She often tries to get chewing gum out of a packet and into her mouth so surreptitiously that no one around her notices. Every time I see this happening, I will, without fail, say loudly, so that our whole group of friends can hear: 'Hey, can I have some gum, please?' I do it just to annoy her. (Yes, I do realise that's not very merciful!)

Open hands

All of us have things we do not want to share, whether they are small and silly or large and understandable. With the world around us screaming that what we have matters – that it reveals how much of a success or failure we are – a lot of us like to keep a tight grip on our stuff.

Maybe that is why God has to tell us to share so often. Through the law of Moses, he told the Israelites not to be 'hard-hearted or tight-fisted', but rather to be 'open-handed', lending freely whatever is needed, and giving 'generously... without a grudging heart' (Deuteronomy 15:7–10, NIV). Through the prophets, he told his people to share their bread with the hungry and their homes with the homeless (Isaiah 58:7). When the crowds asked John the Baptist what they should do, he said: 'Anyone who has two shirts should share with the one who has none, and anyone who has food should do the same' (Luke 3:11, NIV).

The apostle Paul wrote to believers that they should 'share with the Lord's people who are in need' (Romans 12:13, NIV). He told Timothy to command the wealthy 'to do good, to be rich in good works, to be generous and ready to share' (1 Timothy 6:18). The writer to the Hebrews said: 'Do not neglect to do good and to share what you have, for such sacrifices are pleasing to God' (Hebrews 13:16). James warns that it is no good to bless someone with words if we do not accompany that with feeding, clothing and 'giving them the things needed for the body' (James 2:14–17) – he calls that dead faith. And the apostle John puts it just as bluntly when he writes that if we have enough, yet close our hearts to those who are in need, God's love cannot be in us (1 John 3:17, NIV).

From the Old Testament to the New, from the law to the letters, from the prophets to the Messiah, everywhere we look in the Bible we find that God wants us to share what we have.

Jesus looked at the rich young ruler and loved him, but the rich young ruler loved what he had more than the One who had given it to him (Mark 10:17–22). In stark contrast, when Zacchaeus the wealthy tax collector encountered the mercy of Jesus for himself, his immediate, unsolicited response was to offer to give away half of all he owned to people in poverty, and to restore fourfold anything he had gained by fraud (Luke 19:5–10).

An encounter with the mercy of God will affect our finances and loosen our grip on what we have. When we actively choose to cultivate open-handedness rather than wait for God to prise each finger off our precious belongings, we step into a mercy with our material possessions that is a countercultural hallmark of Jesus followers.

People over possessions

It is easy for us to read what Jesus said to the rich and assume those words do not apply to us. Or to fail to heed the warnings of James about living in luxury and self-indulgence (James 5:5), because we compare ourselves to millionaires and billionaires rather than to those in need around us. We forget that smartphones, bottles of wine, holidays, cars, getting our nails done and playing golf belong firmly and fully in the 'luxury' category.

If we want to live lives of radical mercy that reflect the astonishing mercy we have been shown by God, we need to examine how attached we are to what we have, and whether we have let the world confuse us about which goods are essential and which are not. The question is not about how much we have. It is possible for us to have a healthy attitude to our wealth, and it is equally possible to be materialistic with very little. It is not about what we have, but how tethered our hearts are to it.

A sober assessment of our own materialism will open the door for us to make sure that belongings and comfort are not more valuable to us than showing mercy to people in need. This does not mean we will all respond in the same way. John Wesley lived modestly throughout his life; cricketer CT Studd gave away all he had, then moved to China as a missionary; George Cadbury created huge wealth and used it for the benefit of his workers, building a village for them to live in, schools for their children and green spaces for them to enjoy, and pioneering pension schemes and medical support. Cadbury and his family made a lot of money, but used it for the good of those around them who had less.

We are not all called to do exactly the same thing with whatever God has blessed us with, but we are all called to be merciful with what we have, prioritising people above possessions, and ensuring that the wellbeing of others becomes and remains more important to us than what we own.

As followers of God, whatever the size of our bank balance, whether we own a little or a lot, we have the privilege of being rich in mercy, just like our Father.

25

Open lives

Being merciful is not just about sharing what we have; it is also about opening up our lives. In the Bible we see lots of different expressions of mercy in action. For Job, mercy was a demonstration of righteousness. When his friends argued that his suffering must have been brought about by his sin, Job defended his righteousness before God by listing his acts of mercy. He recounted how he had delivered the poor, 'caused the widow's heart to sing for joy', supported the disabled, acted like a father towards those in poverty, and even looked out for strangers to help (Job 29:12–16). Job wept over the hardships of others (Job 30:25). He made all of his resources available to those in need by feeding, clothing and sheltering them (Job 31:16–22). In defending his righteousness, Job reveals himself to be a model of mercy.

For Mordecai, mercy towards those in poverty was an act of worship and celebration of what God had done for his people. Once the Jews had been spared from annihilation thanks to his niece Esther, Mordecai urged them to enjoy a public holiday of feasting, and said that part of their celebrations should include sending 'gifts to the poor' as a way of remembering that God had turned their sorrow into joy (Esther 9:22). The Jewish holiday of Purim still includes giving to those in need today, and even those who are in poverty give to others as part of the celebration.

Acts of mercy are demonstrations of righteousness for Job, and of thanksgiving for deliverance for Mordecai. For Nehemiah, being merciful is both a public and a personal responsibility. He advocated on behalf of those who were starving owing to exploitation, and he went without the food and wine to which he was entitled. Unlike the Pharisees, whom Jesus called out for laying heavy burdens on people while not attending to the weightier matters themselves, Nehemiah acted publicly to see burdens relieved, and personally to ensure that he was not laying heavy burdens on anyone (Nehemiah 5:18).

Welcomed in

Jesus ate at the homes of a wide range of people, but many of us in Western cultures today view our homes as places where we can get away from the outside world, rather than welcoming all sorts of people in. Holidays are times when we bunker down in our nuclear family units. Our sense of homes as hideaways was exacerbated during the coronavirus pandemic, when various lockdowns forced us to retreat to stay safe. We stayed in, and we kept other people out.

We have already seen that Jesus ate with the rich and with the poor. He fed the crowds, and he picked out people such as Zacchaeus the tax collector, inviting himself over for dinner. He broke bread with those he knew would deny and betray him. He ate with those who loved him and those who wished him harm.

Being welcomed into people's homes for meals has been a key part of my own story. The first time I saw food served in separate dishes for meat, vegetables and potatoes was after I became a Christian. I felt anxious and out of my depth when food was set before me in this unfamiliar way, because I didn't know if there were rules I was supposed to follow. Nevertheless, there was something powerful about being welcomed into people's homes.

Even today, as a single woman living on my own, one of the primary ways I experience the mercy of God through my church family is at the dinner table. Before COVID-19 came along, I managed forty-six days in a row being fed by friends, and I was pretty proud of myself for that!

It speaks volumes to people when we share a meal together, because eating with people is about more than food. It's about community, friendship and belonging. Our meal tables can be powerful places where people who feel broken, alone, ashamed or in need can find deep mercy.

Likewise, doing mercy can be the simple act of inviting people into everyday life with us. Aside from during the pandemic, I have joined in for several years with the Christmas Eve meal that is a tradition for a family at my church. The first two or three times, I was astonished to be included in this special family occasion. These days, it is still a privilege to be welcomed in, but I now assume I am invited – usually I will ask one of the family members what time to come, rather than wait to see if they invite me!

Another family at church tell me their plans for Christmas Day, so that if I want to go along I can choose based on what is happening and when. They make it clear that I am welcome to any or all of it, but they will not be offended if I do not come.

To call these invitations acts of mercy might seem too much, but the impact they can have on a person's heart – the sense of belonging and family they can create – are incalculable. Sometimes the ways in which we open up our lives may be an inconvenience to us, but mean the world to the person being included.

Opening up our meal tables is so important because when we eat together and hear each other's stories, our preconceived ideas are often challenged. God can work in our hearts to dislodge prejudices and faulty thinking about others, whether that be about groups or individuals.

Listening and learning

My life is enriched by spending time with people who are not like me. We learn more from people whose life experiences are very different from our own than we do from people who are just like us.

I wonder if this is why Jesus chose disciples who were unlikely to get on well, naturally speaking. The chances are, Peter the fisherman and Matthew the tax collector would have never become friends if Jesus had not put them side by side for three years as they followed him.

Proximity to people who are different from us provides another opportunity for us to grow in mercy towards others. Understanding develops compassion. It is hard to hold on to certain views about people from other nations coming here 'to take our jobs', for example, when you have spent time with a teacher from Bulgaria who tells you about his meagre salary in his homeland, and how there is no chance he could support his children on what he was earning there.

We become increasingly merciful through hearing other people's stories. When I listen to someone talk about their life, their experiences, their trials and their triumphs, it creates space for God to develop compassion in my heart.

This particularly struck me on a trip to San Francisco. I was wandering around on my own, asking God to speak to me about this whole subject of mercy, specifically in regard to the idea of the 'deserving' and 'undeserving' poor. As I was walking and praying, I turned a corner and saw a man holding a cardboard sign that read: 'Why lie? I want beer.'[1]

Intrigued, especially in the light of the prayer I had just prayed, I asked the man about his sign. I didn't know what to make of his honesty. Would people respect him for it, or avoid giving to him knowing what their money was going towards? I might respond to a sign asking for food or shelter, but I didn't want to buy him beer. He told me his story. Years of drug addiction had wrecked all of his relationships, he said. He had received help and support, but each time he left rehab, he had quickly fallen back into his old patterns. He explained that in the last couple of years he had kicked his addiction to crack cocaine, but had replaced it with 'a new poison': alcohol.

As he shared his story, instead of judging him for wanting beer money, I began to feel compassion towards him. Listening provided a platform for my heart to be changed. And that is so often the way. Simply taking the time to listen to someone's story gives the Holy Spirit room to move us from judgement to mercy to action.

Being merciful is about sharing what we have, but we must not limit it to that. Truly doing mercy means going out of our way to support other people. Mercy can be massively inconvenient. Sharing our homes and holidays with people might feel uncomfortable. Helping others to mature in their character or skills may slow us down. Speaking up on behalf of someone else's cause may get us into trouble or harm our reputation. Once when I defended a colleague, the employees who had been bullying her turned on me as well.

Disruptive prayers

If you want to rise to the challenge but are wondering where to begin, start by asking God to bring people across your path, even this week, to whom you can show mercy. Be prepared for Him to push you out of your comfort zone. Sometimes it is the simple prayers we pray that are the most likely to disrupt our lives!

When a friend of mine started praying like this, she found she could no longer go out for a run without bursting into tears as she passed someone who was sleeping on the streets. Prompted by the Holy Spirit, she ran home, made a bacon roll and ran back to give it to the person. This small act became a habit of mercy for the next three years. Once a week she would give out up to a dozen breakfasts on her morning run. She prayed that she would become more merciful, like the Father, and he was quick to answer.

For you, it might feel more difficult. Perhaps God will highlight a family member who drives you to despair, and ask you to cultivate mercy for him or her. Tucked away in Isaiah 58, in the middle of words about injustice and hunger, God says that true fasting includes not hiding away from our own relatives (Isaiah 58:7). It can be easier to show mercy to someone at the local food bank than to someone in our own family.

As you pursue doing mercy, look for ways to join in with others, because we are sharpened when we work together (Proverbs 27:17). If your church runs a mercy ministry, such as a night shelter, food bank or clothing store, how can you get involved? Can you offer some of your time, skills, encouragement or prayers, even if it disrupts your diary or your sense of comfort?

Perhaps the Lord will start to speak to you about your money, possessions, skills, meal table, friendship circle, time or even your home. One of the ways of the kingdom I find less appealing, if I'm honest, is that the more I give, the more God seems to ask of me. But the truth is, everything we have is his anyway. As the apostle Paul puts it: 'What do you have that you did not receive?' (1 Corinthians 4:7).

I am trying not to resist God. I don't want to make him prise my stubborn fingers, one by one, from whatever I am gripping tightly. Instead, I am learning (slowly!) to adopt an open-handed posture, where nothing is off limits to Jesus. He can have anything he wants, as it all came from him anyway. As Oswald Chambers writes of Paul: 'Jesus Christ was always allowed to help Himself to his life.'[2]

Can the same be said of us?

I am a work in progress, but I want to be merciful, just as my Father is merciful. So, with my hands covering my eyes as I hope it won't be too painful, I pray: 'Jesus, help yourself to whatever you want.'

26

A daily habit

Doing mercy isn't just about holding all we have with open hands. It is about cultivating a lifestyle. But mercy is a challenge even in the everyday circumstances of life.

Being merciful is hard when you ask your neighbour if they can keep the noise down – just for the next hour because you have an important call to make, or you cannot get the baby to sleep – and they say no, not caring about your situation one bit.

This happened to me recently. I live in a flat with pretty poor soundproofing between the floors and ceilings, so I often hear conversations taking place below and above me. One set of neighbours is always really accommodating if I am doing a radio interview, for example. But when I recently asked the other set, for the first time, if I could just have half an hour without them dismantling furniture so I could record two conference seminars, the answer was no. I asked if we could compromise and I could have ten minutes to get one done. They said no. Maybe I spend too much time around Christians, but I was surprised.

I wanted to say: 'OK, well I will remember this next time you ask me for something.' But Jesus does not allow me to do that. To be honest, I was pretty annoyed for the rest of the evening that I'm not allowed to react like that! Loving mercy and being merciful mean that I choose not to retaliate, but also that if they come to me tomorrow and ask *me* to keep the noise down, I graciously agree.

This may sound like becoming a doormat, and letting people treat me however they want, but it is putting into practice what Jesus said about turning the other cheek (Matthew 5:39). It is fine for me to stand my ground and ask my neighbour to be reasonable, but mercy does not give me permission to hold a grudge or to retaliate tit for tat. When I indulge the anti-mercy in my heart, it brings out my most childish behaviour. Maturity as a believer looks like turning the other cheek so that I am gazing at Jesus, not glaring at my annoying neighbour. If I am going to imitate anyone in this sort of scenario, it should not be my neighbour, but my Saviour.

Changing the question

Being merciful in the small, everyday things can be so difficult. Your colleague repeatedly misses a deadline, the waiter in the restaurant is grumpy with you, or your friend is half an hour late for the umpteenth time. These are the things that happen every day that can provoke us to moaning to others about people, digging in our heels about how we will treat them in the future, or getting them back somehow.

But mercy is also hard work in the big everyday things. I grew up with a family member who was abusive and deeply unkind. During my adult life, the same relative has at various times wanted to be part of my life and gone months without any contact, once even telling me they had never liked me and no longer wanted anything to do with me.

That is painful. But when I fix my eyes on Jesus rather than this family member and the hurt they have caused me, I find that my question changes from: 'Should I spend time with someone who has wounded me, and sometimes continues to wound me?' to: 'Father, what does it look like to show your mercy here?' The answer might be the same either way, but reframing what we are asking God and ourselves helps us to cultivate loving mercy and being merciful. Sometimes mercy involves walking away. Sometimes the most merciful thing we can do is *not* rescue someone from the consequences of their actions.

Whatever the answer, the fundamental difference between the two questions is heart posture. One is unconcerned with mercy; the other is rooted in wanting to show mercy.

What does it look like for me to show mercy to my noisy neighbour? Quick forgiveness is key, and choosing to bless them if I have opportunity, rather than holding this against them and trying to get back at them when the opportunity arises.

What does it look like for me to show mercy to my unkind relative? Deep, costly forgiveness is hard, but vital – Jesus made this very clear (Matthew 6:14–15, 18:21–35; see also 2 Corinthians 2:5–8; Ephesians 4:31–32; Colossians 3:12–14). We have been forgiven much, therefore we are to forgive as an act of gratitude and obedience, as well as for our own well-being.

I find it helpful (though difficult!) to ask God to bless the people who have hurt me the most. Usually, if it is a recent wound, I pray for them through gritted teeth. But as I press through, wanting to please Jesus and become more like him, I find it becomes easier over time. In his kindness, healing comes that way, too. He binds up my hurting heart. As that happens – and as I 'pour out [my] heart like water [to] the LORD' (Lamentations 2:19) about how I feel, the pain I am in, how I long for justice – I find it becomes easier (though not easy) to get my heart into a posture where I can ask what the merciful response would be.

Mercy is required from us many more times a day than we may have noticed. As we let our hearts be shaped towards mercy by our Father, and as we actively pursue a lifestyle of mercy, we realise there is no shortage of opportunity to show mercy. It is required of us every day. When we embrace it, we discover that there is great joy in cultivating a daily habit of mercy.

27

The mercy loop

We are saved by grace, not by works. Yet, curiously, there are promises connected to how merciful we are. Jesus says plainly: 'Blessed are the merciful, for they shall receive mercy' (Matthew 5:7). It is one of the mysteries of God's mercy that there are promises and principles attached – that those who are merciful will be shown mercy.

I do not pretend to fully understand how this works. The Bible is explicitly clear that we cannot earn God's mercy, that we do not deserve it, and that our salvation is *his* work, not *ours*, 'so that no human being might boast in the presence of God' (1 Corinthians 1:29; Ephesians 2:4–9). I know full well that I have no right to the mercy I have received – that I cannot earn it and do not deserve it – but I have also seen and experienced it to be true that 'great blessings belong to those who show mercy to others' (Matthew 5:7, ERV).

Principles of mercy

One portion of Scripture that puts some flesh onto the bones of this idea of receiving mercy when we give it is Isaiah 58:6–12, where we are told not only what mercy looks like in action, but also of the promises and principles we can take hold of when we act in accordance with God's heart. The context is that the people of God are complaining to him that they are observing their religious duties, but he isn't paying attention (Isaiah 58:3). Through his prophet Isaiah, the Lord explains what true fasting looks like:

Is not this the fast that I choose:
    to loose the bonds of wickedness,
    to undo the straps of the yoke,
to let the oppressed go free,
    and to break every yoke?
Is it not to share your bread with the hungry
    and bring the homeless poor into your house;
when you see the naked, to cover him,
    and not to hide yourself from your own flesh?
Then shall your light break forth like the dawn,
    and your healing shall spring up speedily;
your righteousness shall go before you;
    the glory of the LORD *shall be your rear guard.*
Then you shall call, and the LORD *will answer;*
    you shall cry, and he will say, 'Here I am.'
If you take away the yoke from your midst,
    the pointing of the finger, and speaking wickedness,
if you pour yourself out for the hungry
    and satisfy the desire of the afflicted,
then shall your light rise in the darkness
    and your gloom be as the noonday.
And the LORD *will guide you continually*
    and satisfy your desire in scorched places
    and make your bones strong;
and you shall be like a watered garden,
    like a spring of water,
    whose waters do not fail.
And your ancient ruins shall be rebuilt;
    you shall raise up the foundations of many generations;
you shall be called the repairer of the breach,
    the restorer of streets to dwell in.

In these verses, God reminds his people about what really matters to him, and calls them back – not to religious duties and rules, but to his very heart of mercy.

There is a progression in verse six that shows us that, in the same way that another prophet, Ezekiel, went ankle-deep, then knee-deep, then waist-deep in the river of God (Ezekiel 47), we are to press deeper and deeper into reflecting the heart of God. When we walk in the rivers of God's mercy, we find that we start ankle-deep, loosening the bonds of wickedness. Then we go knee-deep, undoing the ties that are binding people, progressing to waist-deep, where we set the oppressed (or bruised) free. Finally, we find ourselves swimming in the powerful waters of God's mercy when we break every yoke so that chains are broken and cannot be used to hold people down ever again.

But the prophet Isaiah doesn't just call us to release the downtrodden and oppressed. We are also called to use what we have to bless others: our bread, our homes, our clothing, our time. And we are not to do it piecemeal, rationing our good deeds with a little bit here and a little bit there, as and when we can fit it in. Instead, those who worship and serve the Lord are to 'pour [ourselves] out' (Isaiah 58:10, ESV), to 'spend' ourselves (NIV) on behalf of the hungry and afflicted.

We might expect God to say that once we have done these things – broken the chains of the oppressed and devoted ourselves to providing for those in need – their healing shall come, their desires will be satisfied, their gloom will be like the noonday, their ancient ruins shall be rebuilt.

But God doesn't say that.

He says those things will happen to *us*.

Blessed when we bless

God's mercy towards us is so magnificent that when we show mercy to others, even though we are merely doing as we should, we are greatly blessed; often, much more so than those we help.

I have seen this at work in my own life. If you are in the habit of giving to others, I am sure you will have observed the truth of Jesus' words: 'It is more blessed to give than to receive' (Acts 20:35). When we bless others with our finances or resources, we often find that we receive back more abundantly than we have given.

But we are not just blessed financially. When we give our energy to people who have nothing to offer in return – when we are merciful to those whom others might discard, write off, or not have time for – there is a curious spiritual principle at work where we begin to find that our own well-being and emotions are affected.

Doing good does us good.

This is not just a theory; there is research to back it up. Giving our time and energy for the good of others is actually good for our health. It can reduce stress, lower our blood pressure, slow down memory loss, keep us mobile and even lengthen our lives.[1]

After initially being diagnosed with depression when I was nineteen years old, I suffered with it throughout most of my twenties and thirties, going through phases of self-harm in different forms and struggling with suicidal thoughts. Early on, I was prescribed various drugs with varying degrees of success. For a brief spell in my twenties, I was on antidepressants, tranquillisers and sleeping pills, all at the same time. The combination didn't make me feel better; it simply stopped me feeling at all. A number of things have helped over the years, from powerful encounters with Jesus that can change things in an instant, to the slow and painstaking plod of working through deeply entrenched issues with a professional counsellor.

But what has also helped is committing my time and energy to the good of others whose lives are harder than mine. As I have poured myself out, my gloom has become like the noonday – not always, not instantly, not permanently – but my experience has been that God's word is true. As I turn my attention to satisfying the desires of the afflicted, I find that my desires begin to be satisfied, too.

Being merciful is good for us.

Pour out, drink in

But it's not a magic formula. Putting in a shift at your local food bank probably won't make your depression disappear. God is not a vending machine, where we put in some breaking-of-the-yoke and a bit of bread-sharing, and in return we get out speedy healing, satisfied desires and the nickname 'restorer of streets' (Isaiah 58:12).

They are not cast-iron promises in the sense that if we do 'x' we will definitely receive 'y'. But they are principles of mercy that we can pursue – principles that start to work powerfully in our own lives when we give ourselves to becoming more and more like our Father of mercies.

God delights in blessing us when we show mercy. The glorious principle at work is that, as we reflect his mercy, compassion, kindness and steadfast love to those around us, the Lord blesses us in all our work (Deuteronomy 15:10), protects us from our enemies, restores us from sickness (Psalm 41:3), lightens our darkness, guides us, satisfies us, strengthens us and rebuilds us, even as we rebuild others (Isaiah 58:8–12).

In many respects, it is like a beautiful, never-ending loop of mercy. We receive it abundantly, afresh from God each day, and we pour it out abundantly to others. Jesus promises to bless us with mercy when we are merciful (Matthew 5:7).

So let's wade out into the depths of God's mercy, bringing freedom to the bound and provision to the poorest, knowing that as we bring that mercy to others and focus our attention on doing them good, we are at the same time doing ourselves good by bathing in the precious waters of God's mercy that will transform our lives too.

Conclusion

'Tis mercy all

The mercy of God is immense. It is rich, relentless and unrestrained. I cannot exaggerate the mercy of God. Even if I use all the superlatives I know, I will still fail to do justice to it. It is magnificent. Some days it feels as if I will never get my head around the fact that God is acquainted with all my ways, and yet has not treated me as my sins deserve. He has saved me – not because of anything righteous I have done, but 'according to his own mercy' (Titus 3:5).

I contributed not one single righteous act to my salvation.

'Tis mercy all.

My sins, once like crimson, are now nailed to the cross. Jesus has taken the punishment and clothed me in his righteousness. He has paid my ransom and saved me to the uttermost.

'Tis mercy all.

And now I am secure. Christ Jesus has made me his own (Philippians 3:12), and no one can snatch me out of his hand (John 10:28–28). I belong to him. He has bound himself to me in covenant commitment. I am his today, and forevermore.

'Tis mercy all!

Dwelling deeply on the mercy of God towards us leads us into worship. When we realise we can come boldly to the throne of our Father and find all the mercy we need (Hebrews 4:16) – abundant mercy that he delights in showing to us – it causes our hearts to soar in gratitude. His mercies towards us are tender, but mighty. When we wander, it is God's mercy that follows us and draws us back to wonder.

When we gaze on God's mercy, we are 'astonished beyond measure' (Mark 7:37) at how far God would go to win us for himself; how committed to us he is; how gloriously forgiving, patient, loving and kind he is. How utterly different God is from all we see around us and within us.

Can it really be so? When we stare our objections and doubts full in the face, we find there is yet more richness to his mercy than we dared to hope, and we disbelieve for joy (Luke 24:41), marvelling at how wonderful God is, how relentless he is in his pursuit of us.

'Tis mercy all, immense and free; For, O my God, it found out me!

'Mercy is a beautiful and unusual thing,' writes Amy Orr-Ewing.[1]

Worship is the right and natural response to the mercy of God.

But worship must not be our only response.

Maturing in mercy

'In view of God's mercy' we are to live holy lives, pleasing God not by being conformed to the pattern of this world (Romans 12:1–2, NIV), which lacks mercy and is largely anti-mercy, but by being conformed to the image of his Son (Romans 8:29, NIV). It is what he predestined us for. We were set apart before we were born (Jeremiah 1:5, NIV), to be transformed into the image of Jesus one degree at a time (2 Corinthians 3:18).

We please God when we hope in his mercy (Psalm 147:11, NKJV), but followers of Jesus are required not just to hope in it but to 'love mercy' and to 'be merciful'. A mature view of the incredible mercy of God towards us will transform our thinking and propel us into action.

Loving mercy is hard.

Doing mercy is hard.

But we have the amazing privilege of being just like our Father, representing him to the world around us, which does not know mercy and does not know God.

Conclusion

It is a high calling that requires deep work.

It starts with an excavation in our hearts of the ways in which we have failed to love mercy. All the attitudes and thinking we have taken in from the polarised cancel culture around us need rooting out. Instead of blame and shame, we need to rediscover the art of forgiveness and the heart of redemption.

We cultivate a love for mercy in our hearts by giving the Holy Spirit freedom to reshape our thinking. It might put us at odds with the normal thinking of our society. It might put us at odds with others in the Church. It might even put us at odds with ourselves, as we experience the pain of allowing God to renew our minds and stretch our thoughts, so that they become more like his.

Once we delight in mercy, not just for ourselves but for others too – including those we consider to be undeserving, and even our enemies – we can start to imitate God. Attitudes turn to actions. Merciful thoughts become merciful deeds.

Christians are called to be mercy-bringers. When we become hypervigilant for signs of God's abundant mercy at work in our lives, and when we intentionally seek to align our hearts with his, we quickly experience the great privilege and joy of reflecting the Father to those around us.

Mercy is one of the distinctives of the Christian faith. It is one of the characteristics we should be known for, yet so often we are known for being judgemental rather than merciful. We have been shown such overwhelming mercy; how can we not show it to others (Matthew 18:33)?

We are called to be countercultural, radical, even revolutionary, in a society that has no mercy and has learned to despise it.

The world needs us to be the Jesus-imitating mercy-bringers we were created to be. We must point people to Jesus because, while we can offer practical and temporal mercy, he is the only One who offers ultimate mercy.

Conclusion

The gap between the mercy we have received and the mercy we show urgently needs to shrink.

When we are merciful, people are drawn to Jesus.

When we are merciful, our lives glorify God.

So, in a world in which mercy is hard to find, let's stand out. Let's point people to Jesus by *loving* mercy and *doing* mercy. Our worshipful, God-honouring response to the wonderful mercy we have received is to be merciful, just as our Father is merciful.

Notes

Epigraph

1 Wesley, C., 'And Can It Be That I Should Gain?' (public domain).
2 Packer, J. I. and Vanhoozer, K. J., *Knowing God: With study guide* (London: Hodder & Stoughton, 1993), p. 138.

Introduction

1 I originally wrote about Jo's parents extending mercy to the driver who killed their daughter in the May 2022 edition of *Inspiring Women Every Day*, published by Waverley Abbey Resources. Other ideas about the mercy of God also first appeared in writing in brief form in that devotional.
2 The ESV translates *khesed* as 'mercy' in Psalm 23:6 and both *khanan* and *rakhamim* (the noun form of *rakhum*) as 'mercy' in Psalm 51:1, while the NKJV translates *khesed*, *khanan* and *rakham* as 'mercy' in Psalms 4:1, 102:13 and throughout 136. All three Hebrew words appear in Exodus 34:6, where God reveals himself to Moses as 'merciful and gracious… abounding in steadfast love'.
3 Thanks to my friend, the author and theologian Andrew Wilson, for helping me with the Greek and Hebrew, and particularly for his succinct explanation of the different words for 'mercy' in a Jubilee+ 'Monday Mercy' video: https://jubilee-plus.org/monday-mercy/1247/monday-mercy-95-confrontational-mercy.

1

1 Storms, S., *A Dozen Things God Did with Your Sin (And Three Things He'll Never Do)*, (Wheaton, IL: Crossway, 2022) p. 94.
2 Ortlund, D. C., *Gentle and Lowly: The heart of Christ for sinners and sufferers* (Carol Stream, IL: Crossway, 2020) p. 172.

2

1 I'm grateful to Amy Orr-Ewing for her keynote talk and seminar on forgiveness and reconciliation at the National Parliamentary Prayer

Breakfast in Westminster in June 2023, which helped to clarify some of my thinking about how our culture views justice and mercy.

3

1 Gibson, D. *The Lord of Psalm 23: Jesus our shepherd, companion, and host* (Wheaton, IL: Crossway, 2023), p. 128.

2 Ortlund, D. C., *In the Lord I Take Refuge: 150 daily devotions through the Psalms* (Wheaton, IL: Crossway, 2021), p. 298.

3 This is one example of where the word *khesed* can be translated as 'mercy' as accurately as 'steadfast love'. For an example of where Jesus himself translated *khesed* as 'mercy', see Matthew 9:13 and 12:7, where the Greek word *eleos* (which is always translated 'mercy') is used for the Hebrew word *khesed* when quoting Hosea 6:6.

4 King Canute (also known as Cnut or Cnut the Great) was the Danish king of England from 1016 to 1035. Today, he is mostly remembered for allegedly sitting enthroned on the beach and trying to command the waves to stay back, though there is no historical evidence that this really happened.

5 Gibson, D., *The Lord of Psalm 23*, pp. 121–23.

4

1 Ortlund, D. C., *Gentle and Lowly*, p. 27.

2 Some scholars believe these two men are the same person, but this is unlikely, as Mark 14 has Simon the leper's home located in Bethany, while Luke 7 has Jesus travelling from Capernaum to Nain and being in that region when visiting Simon the Pharisee's home. Either way, the point remains valid that there are some people most of us would be happy to see Jesus eating with, and some we would not.

3 Similar wording to some parts of this paragraph and the one above first appeared in *The Myth of the Undeserving Poor*, which I co-authored with Martin Charlesworth (Surbiton: Grosvenor House, 2014), p. 54.

5

1 Keller, T., *My Rock; My Refuge: A year of daily devotions in the Psalms* (London: Hodder & Stoughton, 2015), p. 283.

9

1 Bojorquez, M. and Powell, T. B., '"Justice wasn't served": Parkland families outraged as shooter is spared death sentence by Florida jury', CBS News, 14 October 2022: https://www.cbsnews.com/news/parkland-families-outraged-shooter-spared-death-sentence-florida-jury (accessed 7 December 2023).

2 'Parkland school shooter to be sentenced to life without parole', *The Guardian*, 2 November 2022: https://www.theguardian.com/us-news/2022/nov/02/parkland-school-shooter-sentencing-life-without-parole (accessed 16 April 2023).

3 Buckler, L., 'Gran of Parkland school shooting victim, 14, tells "monster" he will "burn in hell"', *The Mirror*, 1 November 2022: https://www.mirror.co.uk/news/us-news/gran-parkland-school-shooting-victim-28381434 (accessed 16 April 2023).

4 Cabral, S. and Ostasiewicz, A., 'Parkland shooting verdict: "I'm as stunned as the day Luke was killed"', BBC News, 14 October 2022: https://www.bbc.co.uk/news/world-us-canada-63251245 (accessed 16 April 2023).

5 Obviously, not all cultures define murder in the same way. Killing someone for no reason is wrong everywhere, though some cultures would accept reasons that would be morally reprehensible and illegal in others. For example, honour killings are murder according to the laws of many countries, though they would be viewed as acceptable and legitimate in some nations.

6 See Matthew 22:16, where a variant of this Greek word is used to describe Jesus as unable to be swayed by people, and then Acts 10:34, Romans 2:11, Ephesians 6:9, Colossians 3:25 and 1 Peter 1:17 for other uses of the word and its variants to inform us that God does not show partiality.

10

1 Ortlund, D. C., *Gentle and Lowly*, p. 148.

11

1 Spurgeon, C. H., 'A Happy Christian', The Spurgeon Center, 1867: https://www.spurgeon.org/resource-library/sermons/a-happy-christian/#flipbook (accessed 29 November 2023).

13

1 Henry, M., 'Matthew Henry's Commentary', Bible Hub: https://biblehub.com/commentaries/mhc/isaiah/54.htm (accessed 29 November 2023).

2 Piper, J., 'Call Me Husband, Not Baal', Desiring God, 26 December 1982: https://www.desiringgod.org/messages/call-me-husband-not-baal (accessed 29 November 2023).

Part 3 introduction

1 Nouwen, H., 'You Belong to God', Henri Nouwen Society, 11 January 2023: https://henrinouwen.org/meditations/you-belong-to-god (accessed 25 August 2023).

15

1 See 2 Samuel 9:3, ESV, JUB, GNT and WYC. As mentioned in the Introduction, *khesed* can be translated as 'lovingkindness', 'kindness' or 'mercy', and is translated as 'mercy' in most English versions of the Bible in one verse or another.

2 Haslam, G., *The Jonah Complex* (Kent: River Publishing, 2011), p. 160.

3 See, for example, 'The Welfies: Brits with talent for playing the benefits system', *The Sun*, 15 January 2015: https://www.thesun.co.uk/archives/news/11453/the-welfies (accessed 8 May 2023).

16

1 '14 Billy Graham Quotes That Helped Shape American Christianity', Relevant, 21 February 2019: https://relevantmagazine.com/faith/14-billy-graham-quotes-helped-shape-american-christianity (accessed 21 August 2023).

2 Charlesworth, M. and Williams, N., *The Myth of the Undeserving Poor: A Christian response to poverty in Britain today* (Surbiton: Grosvenor House, 2014), pp. 41–7.

3 Bonhoeffer, D., *Letters and Papers from Prison*, quoted in Watkin, C., *Biblical Critical Theory: How the Bible's unfolding story makes sense of modern life and culture* (Grand Rapids, MI: Zondervan Academic, 2022), p. 128.

17

1 Virgo, T., Twitter, 20 May 2022: https://twitter.com/TerryVirgo/
status/1527522554897891328 (accessed 29 November 2023).

2 This idea is famously expressed by Aleksandr Solzhenitsyn in *The
Gulag Archipelago* (London: Vintage Classics, 2018), but is taken here
from Watkin, C., *Biblical Critical Theory: How the Bible's unfolding
story makes sense of modern life and culture* (Grand Rapids, MI:
Zondervan Academic, 2022), p. 129.

18

1 'The dazzling crown that will make a king', BBC News, 5 May 2023:
https://www.bbc.co.uk/news/resources/idt-5136bea2-40b8-45bf-83be-
e06babcbc2bf (accessed 6 May 2023).

2 'The dazzling crown which sat on the Queen's coffin', BBC news, 19
September 2022: https://www.bbc.co.uk/news/uk-england-62906194
(accessed 6 May 2023).

3 Some of the content in this chapter was originally written in brief form
for the May 2022 edition of *Inspiring Women Every Day* (Waverley
Abbey Resources). Coincidentally, in that devotional my thoughts on
being 'crowned with mercy' were written for 6 May 2022, exactly a year
before the coronation of King Charles III. Some information about
crowns was gleaned from the Tower of London website: hrp.org.uk/
tower-of-london/history-and-stories/the-crown-jewels (accessed 25
November 2021).

19

1 This lovely phrase is taken from Segal, M., 'Mercy Swallows Any
Sorrow: Struggling beside a sea of blessing', Desiring God, 31 May
2023: https://www.desiringgod.org/articles/mercy-swallows-any-sorrow
(accessed 29 November 2023).

2 'Official Singles Chart on 4/4/2010: 4 April 2010 – 10 April 2010',
Official Charts: https://www.officialcharts.com/charts/singles-
chart/20100404/7501 (accessed 30 November 2023).

3 Chesterton, G. K., *The Scandal of Father Brown* (London: Penguin,
2014).

20

1 In his *Straight to the Heart of Matthew* commentary, Phil Moore points out that Matthew 25 'continues directly on from 24:3, where the disciples came to Jesus *privately*' (London: Monarch, 2010), p. 227.

21

1 I am indebted to Martin Charlesworth for many of the reflections in this chapter. Martin founded Jubilee+, and together we co-authored three books on a Christian response to poverty: *The Myth of the Undeserving Poor: A Christian response to poverty in Britain today* (Surbiton: Grosvenor House, 2014); *A Church for the Poor: Transforming the Church to reach the poor in Britain today* (Colorado Springs, CO: David C. Cook, 2017); and *A Call to Act: Building a poverty-busting lifestyle* (Colorado Springs, CO: David C. Cook, 2020).

22

1 Watkin, C., *Biblical Critical Theory*, pp. 380–1.

2 The *Daily Mail*, 17 February 1997, pp. 6–7.

3 '"If I drink again it'll kill me": Life expectancy in England's coastal towns is 10 years lower than inland', Sky News, 3 March 2023: https://news.sky.com/story/if-i-drink-again-itll-kill-me-life-expectancy-in-englands-coastal-towns-is-10-years-lower-than-inland-12823817 (accessed 10 June 2023).

23

1 Lest we fall into the trap of thinking it is only people on low incomes who use credit cards and get into debt of various kinds, the reality is that those on higher incomes are more likely to have a credit card and to pay off only the minimum they owe, rather than clear the debt or even make substantial headway in paying it off. See: 'Household debt inequalities', Office for National Statistics, 4 April 2016: https://www.ons.gov.uk/peoplepopulationandcommunity/personalandhouseholdfinances/debt/articles/householddebtinequalities/2016-04-04; and Hood, A., Joyce, R. and Sturrock, D., 'Problem debt and low-income households', Institute for Fiscal Studies, 16 January 2018: https://ifs.org.uk/publications/

problem-debt-and-low-income-households (both accessed 2 June 2023). Every four-and-a-half minutes, someone in England and Wales is declared insolvent or bankrupt, and every three hours someone's home is repossessed. See: 'The Money Statistics May 2023', The Money Charity: https://themoneycharity.org.uk/money-statistics/may-2023 (accessed 2 June 2023).

2 Charlesworth M. and Williams, N., *A Call to Act*, pp. 104–05.

25

1 I originally wrote about this in *The Myth of the Undeserving Poor*, co-authored with Martin Charlesworth, pp. 104–05.

2 Chambers, O., 24 February entry in *My Utmost for His Highest*, updated edn (Grand Rapids, MI: Discovery House Books, 1995).

27

1 Examples of reports on the studies that have demonstrated this include: Konrath, S., Fuhrel-Forbis, A., Lou, A. and Brown, S., 'Motives for Volunteering Are Associated With Mortality Risk in Older Adults', University of Michigan and Stony Brook University Medical Center: https://www.apa.org/pubs/journals/releases/hea-31-1-87.pdf; Karlis, N., 'Why Doing Good is Good for the Do-Gooder', *The New York Times*, 26 October 2017: https://www.nytimes.com/2017/10/26/well/mind/why-doing-good-is-good-for-the-do-gooder.html; 'Kindness Matters Guide', Mental Health Foundation: https://www.mentalhealth.org.uk/explore-mental-health/kindness/kindness-matters-guide (all accessed 14 December 2023).

Conclusion

1 Orr-Ewing, A., *Mary's Voice*, (New York: Worthy Publishing, 2023), p. 64,